A MARYKNOLL
LITURGICAL YEAR

A MARYKNOLL LITURGICAL YEAR

Reflections on the Readings for Year C

Edited by
Judy Coode and Kathy McNeely

ORBIS BOOKS
Maryknoll, New York 10545

Founded in 1970, Orbis Books endeavors to publish works that enlighten the mind, nourish the spirit, and challenge the conscience. The publishing arm of the Maryknoll Fathers and Brothers, Orbis seeks to explore the global dimensions of the Christian faith and mission, to invite dialogue with diverse cultures and religious traditions, and to serve the cause of reconciliation and peace. The books published reflect the views of their authors and do not represent the official position of the Maryknoll Society. To learn more about Maryknoll and Orbis Books, please visit our website at www.maryknollsociety.org.

Published by Orbis Books, Box 302, Maryknoll, NY 10545-0302.

Manufactured in the United States of America

Library of Congress Cataloging-in-Publication Data
    A Maryknoll liturgical year : reflections on the readings for year C /
edited by Judy Coode and Kathy McNeely.
        p.   cm.
    Includes index.
    ISBN 978-1-57075-980-2 (pbk.)
    1. Church year meditations. 2. Bible – Meditations. 3. Catholic Church.
Lectionary for Mass (U.S.). Year C. I. Coode, Judy. II. McNeely, Kathy.
BX2170.C55M38 2012
242'.3 – dc23   2012011986

Contents

Preface

As Maryknoll missioners read scripture, their mission experiences—crossing into a new culture, sharing life with new communities—bring fresh meanings of the texts to light. The reflections in the pages that follow describe life in its fullest—sharing the deep pain and struggle that people endure, as well as the hope for "a new heaven and a new earth."

In a world where those who drive the global economy are blind to the grave physical and moral consequences of ignoring Earth's natural limits, scores of Maryknoll sisters, priests, brothers, and lay missioners living in resource-poor and indigenous communities have embraced the principle of sufficiency. Reflecting on the words of scripture read from their unique vantage point, Maryknollers describe how people cope with climate changes that have forced them to move or to give up livelihoods and homeland; they celebrate the solutions people have employed and rejoice in the places where they find hope for the future of the planet.

Maryknollers around the world celebrate diversity as an enriching contribution to inclusive security—even as many in the United States express a desire to exclude those who are different from themselves. Maryknoll missioners around the world celebrate the fact that they are warmly welcomed into the communities in spite of differences in appearance, language, and culture. Missioners often accompany communities struggling with racist practices and tell stories of how looking at "the other" with new and compassionate eyes changed community life for the better. These are the kinds of stories elevated in the reflections included in this book: stories of reconciliation, of interreligious collaboration; stories of ways in which groups have overcome their differences to take on projects that serve the common good.

As it enters into its second century of service to the world, the Maryknoll community celebrates the diversity of gifts offered by other nations and cultures and continues to work shoulder to shoulder with others to build a world where peace and sustainable security are possible. In that new world, immigrant communities feel welcomed and natural resources are not treated as unequally divided spoils that provoke conflict but are used for the common good. It was a privilege to work with the many Maryknoll missioners who contributed these reflections. We hope that in them readers find that the word of God is broken open in new ways.

—Judy Coode and Kathy McNeely

First Sunday of Advent

Sr. Janet Hockman, MM

Nepal

Jeremiah 33:14–16; Psalm 25:4–5, 8–10, 14;
First Thessalonians 3:12–4:2; Luke 21:25–28, 34–36

The days are surely coming, says the LORD, when I will fulfill the promise I made to the house of Israel and the house of Judah.
—*Jeremiah 33:14*

A lot of life happens on rooftops in Nepal. Grains are winnowed and herbs are dried in due season, clothes are sunned, games played. Daily prayers are offered there with conch shells sounded, tinkling bells from Hindu neighbors, and the scent of incense offered from Buddhist friends. I looked down from our rooftop each morning to see what else the day might hold. Were the microvans and three-wheeled "tuk-tuks" still in parking lots? Were the students in the boarding school next door doing their 6:00 a.m. exercises and ending with the chanting of "om"? Were the plastic pouches of milk delivered to the local stalls and tea shops? Was it to be an "ordinary" day or had word trickled out through the night of another strike? Is it a valley strike or a nationwide one? Which group called it?

Strike days have an eerie quietness as they begin. Webs of mobile phone connections form for "listening into the day though": where are tires burning, bricks being thrown, vehicles torched, and rallies blocking traffic? Danger may lurk; good judgment is called for. Tensions are internalized and hyper-vigilance squeezes, uninvited, into individuals of all ages and society as a whole. Who is safe? What can be planned and happily anticipated? Such daily inconsistencies erode trust and fortify insecurity for an entire nation. Pacts of military restrictions and arms confinement have been broken. The Peace Accord is bypassed. Admonitions and warnings come from outside, from countries with political and economic interests, from UN representatives and human rights groups, international nongovernmental organizations, leaders of ethnic groups, and sometimes timid voices of religious leaders. How greatly is a prophet needed, voicing truth to which a general response is "Ah, *yes!* This is the life we want." This is always waiting for life.

What is sustainable peace and security? When it is missing, life is robbed. As Advent begins, Jeremiah sets a stance for us: *See! Behold!* Look and be attentive. . . . It takes time, it involves focused intention. Who among us remembers to notice what is missing, what is absent, as well as what is before us? Noticing something missing is an awareness of things known, things dreamed of, hoped for, or promised. Jeremiah names for us things so longed for: fulfilled promises, honesty, integrity, being saved, and dwelling in confidence. These things are of God. They are not new; they have been God-promised and hoped for throughout all of history. For Nepal, as a country, they were expected from dethroned royalty, awaited in a new prime minister, and intended to be written into a first constitution. Their absence leaves the country in a state of insecurity and continued wondering about the possibility of peace.

How does a gaze shift? Where is God, seen and unseen? When do we know ourselves be-held by God and be-holding of God wherever we are? See, in these days that are coming, how we are called upon to help make God's love present and known. Today's passage from Luke's Gospel is brief and clear: Watch yourselves. . . . Stay awake . . . for the strength to survive all that is going to happen . . . and to stand with confidence before the Son of Man.

See! Our eyes, and the eyes of much of the world, have already been focused on dishonesty, depravity, destruction, disaster. We have been awakened to know what is and what is missing. Seeing calls us to responsibility. *Be-hold*, be-holding this Advent the promises of God, the hope of God—not in clenched protectiveness but in gestures of expansive hope for the days that are coming. . . . Jeremiah knew God so powerfully in his own life that he spoke for a future for others to know such love and mercy.

This Advent may we live into the message of 1 Thessalonians by making more and more progress in the kind of life we are meant to live (4:1). What do you see? Who do you see that needs a word of promise, of hope, of peace, of courage, of strength, of faith, of knowing and wanting God among us?

Feast of the Immaculate Conception (December 8)

Sr. Anne Callahan, MM

Guatemala

Genesis 3:9–15, 20; Psalm 98:1–4; Ephesians 1:3–6, 11–12; Luke 1:26–28

Then Mary said, "Here am I, the servant of the Lord; let it be with me according to your word."   —*Luke 1:38*

Today we celebrate the feast of Mary, mother and sister of us all, under the title of the Immaculate Conception. The words "Immaculate Conception" tell us that Holy Wisdom brought forth for our world a very special woman who would give birth to Jesus, the Son of God. We heard in the Gospel that Mary accepted this role by responding to the angel: "Here am I, the servant of the Lord." The title Immaculate Conception denotes that Mary is unique among all persons in that she was conceived without original sin. It is a very lofty title. But note how Mary responded to the angel, "Here am I, servant of the Lord." The title, Immaculate Conception, is lofty and grand. Mary's humility in the scene with the angel is profound.

This is why this feast is so important in the church year. God chose to begin the Christian story through Mary saying, "Yes, I am God's servant."

My mission experience was among very poor women in Guatemala. I recall how December 8 came and went each year in our parish in an extremely marginalized area of Guatemala City. Few people attended Mass on that day, which was surprising because Sunday Mass was always well attended. I knew that the people, especially the women, loved and respected

Mary. Four days after December 8, they would celebrate the feast of Our Lady of Guadalupe; then they would prepare for Christmas with the nine-day remembrance of Mary and Joseph seeking a place to stay in Bethlehem, a custom called *Las Posadas*. But it did not seem comfortable or attractive for them to know Mary as the Immaculate Conception. This was an aspect of the church too elevated, too far away from their personal experience.

They could much more easily identify with Mary mother of the crucified one and with the title "Our Lady of Sorrows." They were mothers, after all, and were living in shacks on invaded land, where many had come to escape the violence of the thirty-year civil war that had produced thousands of refugees, thousands of disappeared and killed, the worst of which took place during the decade of the 1980s.

Finally, a peace accord that ended the war was signed on December 29, 1996. The process and struggle to come to the peace accords had taken ten years. Negotiations languished from the mid-1980s through the early 1990s, so there was much hope in Guatemala during the days following the peace ceremonies.

Knowing that a real peace would be a long project the Catholic Church had initiated a massive nationwide project, called "Recovery of Historical Memory," to bring forth testimony from war victims and to name names. Teams spread out through many dioceses to collect stories of those victimized by the war. But Bishop Juan Gerardi, whose office had led the project, was murdered two days after the project's final results were presented. It was shocking, but also a testament to the fact that peace does not come easily. Any war can live on in the hearts of those affected by its violence.

Think of the numbers of people in our world today, especially the women, who, like Mary, are still suffering the loss of a son or daughter who died in a recent war. They bear the cross every day. They are women and men of the United States, of Iraq, of Afghanistan, who remember and who wonder when peace will really come.

In Guatemala, violence did not end with the peace accords. During these past few years, street violence, gangs, and killing of young women have increased significantly.

On January 1, 2006, I picked up the *New York Times*, and to my surprise, on page 10, I saw a picture of Guadalupe, one of the women I knew from the parish where I had worked. She was mentioned in this article, titled "Guatemala Bleeds in Vise of Gangs and Vengeance," because she was searching at the morgue every Monday morning, hoping to find her son. He had become involved in gangs and was missing and feared murdered. This was ten years after the signing of the last peace accord, and this violence was sown by all the years of a civil war.

We honor Mary, under the title of the Immaculate Conception and on all of her feasts, indeed, every day we are called to work and pray for peaceful solutions to our conflicts, peaceful ways to heal the wounds of our world. Holy Mary, Mother of God, pray for us sinners, now, and at the hour of our death. Our Lady, Queen of Peace, pray for us. Amen.

Second Sunday of Advent

Barbara Fraser, former Maryknoll lay missioner

Peru

Baruch 5:1–9; Psalm 126:1–6; Philippians 1:4–6, 8–11;
Luke 3:1–6

May those who sow in tears reap with shouts of joy.
                                        —Psalm 126:5

Every year, high in the Andes Mountains of Peru, tens of
thousands of pilgrims make an arduous trek to a valley nearly
fifteen thousand feet above sea level. There at the foot of a glacier, they perform traditional dances and pray before an image
of Jesus that marks the spot where the Christ child appeared to
a Quechua boy who was tending his family's animals.

Elderly pilgrims remember when the ice and snow were
practically at the foot of the mountain. Now the glacier is high
up the mountainside. Over the past few decades, the ice has
retreated rapidly. For the pilgrims—Quechua-speaking farmers who herd llamas in the high valleys and plant potatoes and
grain to feed their families—the disappearing glacier is a wor-
risome sign.

Throughout the Andes, people see signs that the climate is
changing. Carmina Sicusta, who lives in a tiny village called
Amaru, points to fields of grain high up a mountainside. Those
crops used to grow only at low elevations. Warmer tempera-
tures are causing the tundra-like pastures on the mountaintops
to shrink, leaving less room for livestock to graze. The glaciers
in the mountains above her village have disappeared. She worries that water will become scarce and she will have trouble
raising food to feed her children.

In the Andes Mountains, water is life. Rains fall from November to March, during the growing season. In the dry months, however, people depend on glaciers, which slowly release water, irrigating pastures where animals graze and feeding streams that provide water for drinking and washing. As the glaciers disappear, the pastures dry up, and neighbors begin to fight over access to the remaining pastures and streams. Some cannot continue to make a living from the land. They migrate to cities, where they face hardship and discrimination, because they have little formal education and do not speak Spanish well.

Farmers in the Andes see the world they have known collapsing around them, because of the changing climate. What they feel is probably similar to what the Israelites felt when they were in exile, or what the Jews of John the Baptist's time felt under foreign occupation. They lived in a time of uncertainty, had little control over events, and did not know if they could promise their children a better future.

Today's readings reminded them—and remind us—of God's faithfulness and the promise of salvation. But the readings also remind us that God calls us to action, to prepare the way for salvation.

Baruch reassures his people that God—who has the power to make difficult ways smooth—has not forgotten them. The people can shed their cloak of mourning and rejoice as their children return from the distant corners of Earth. God will level the mountains and fill in the valleys, smoothing the way for the people to return to God. That hope is echoed in today's psalm, which promises that "those who sow in tears will reap with shouts of joy."

That promise is repeated in the Gospel by John the Baptizer, the "voice crying out in the desert," who urges his listeners to repent and open themselves to God's saving grace. But John also calls us to action: "Prepare the way of the Lord," he says, "make straight his paths." The promise of salvation is ours, too. But what must we do to prepare? How can we make the paths straight?

Paul provides part of the answer in today's epistle. He urges the Philippians to grow in love, knowledge, and perception, so that they can "discern what is of value." His words are as true now as they were for the early Christians.

Advent is a time for preparation, for reflection, for discerning what is of value. It is a time for us to examine the crooked paths in our world and seek ways to make them straight, so they lead us and others to salvation. As we prepare, we must tune our ears to the voices crying out in the wilderness. Who are those voices today? What are they saying? Are we ready to listen to them?

Some of the voices come from distant corners of the world, from people whose lives are precarious, people who are unprotected against the upheaval caused by a changing climate. Quechua farmers in the Andes are trying to keep their farms and feed their families despite the changes. They are planting new crops, digging reservoirs to hold water in the dry season, even welcoming tourists into their villages to share their lives and provide another source of income, in case unpredictable weather ruins their harvest.

Can we listen to their voices and learn from them? Can we learn to live more simply, as they do, using our resources wisely, taking only what we really need and restoring the balance of the natural world so farmers half a world away can stay on their land and not be forced to migrate to cities—to go into exile like the people of Israel?

Advent reminds us of God's promise, but it also calls us to "prepare the way of the Lord, to make straight the paths," for our salvation and for the well-being of our sisters and brothers around the world. Only then can we be assured that "those who go out weeping, bearing the seed for sowing, shall come home with shouts of joy, carrying their sheaves."

Third Sunday of Advent

Marj Humphrey, former Maryknoll lay missioner

Kenya and Sudan

Zephaniah 3:14–18; Isaiah 12:2–6; Philippians 4:4–7;
Luke 3:10–18

Rejoice in the Lord always; again I will say, Rejoice. Let your gladness be known to everyone. The Lord is near.
—Philippians 4:4–5

There is no mistaking the theme that runs throughout the readings for today's Eucharistic celebration, from Zephaniah to Isaiah to St. Paul: "Rejoice!!" "Be glad and exult!" "Sing joyfully!" Each writer proclaims, from his own perspective, that what is to come is worth shouting about, is indeed worth singing about, is truly worth celebrating. They are speaking to those who are impoverished, those who have "further misfortune to fear." They speak to those full of anxiety, who need hope for peace in their lives and peace in their societies. And the source of this joy is the coming of the Lord your God in your midst.

The most extreme poverty I witnessed in my years in Africa was in Southern Sudan in the midst of the civil war there. Working in camps for displaced people, we had seen the cruelest, most miserable kind of poverty and suffering. Our clinic at times had been the ultimate destination of people fleeing the horrors and starvation of this war. There we saw, firsthand, indescribably malnourished children, with stick-like arms and legs so thin they could not hold themselves up, let alone lift their heads when they were finally offered some nourishment. At other times, the camp clinic was the refuge sought by terrified mothers with their children, fleeing bombs and landmines. One day four men who had been out hunting in the forest looking for food for their families were hit with napalm by a low-flying helicopter whose pilot mistook them for "rebels," leaving them horribly burned and disfigured.

We lived in fear there, always listening for the drone of an approaching bomber, the spiraling whistle of the bomb careening toward the ground. One afternoon I found myself huddled with a handful of women and children, facedown, in a fox hole as a MiG bomber strafed our camp and clinic. Bombs exploded around us, as the earth shook and screams surrounded us. Next to me huddled a small boy, maybe ten years old, repeating his mantra, "*Rabbuna fi, Rabbuna fi*": God is here, God is here—sheer, naked belief and hope of "God in our midst."

Who, in this land, could ever shout for joy, "Be glad and exult"? And yet, I found myself at Christmastime experiencing a joy I could never have imagined. As we gathered on Christmas Eve, I marveled at the brilliantly starlit night and wondered if one of those stars was also the same one shining over Bethlehem. There was much joyful chatter and laughter as people who had walked for hours to celebrate their Hope began forming a procession. We would begin by processing behind the cross, decorated with the only festive material we had—blue toilet paper from the mission!

As we began our walk, I was suddenly taken aback, seeing people who had become part of my daily life in a different light, in a cumulative view. For now I saw myself surrounded by broken bodies, legs distorted from polio; limbs twisted from poorly treated, poorly healed fractures; callused stumps that are the feet of lepers; and young amputees with limbs lost to bombs and landmines—one man crawling on the ground with his hands, dragging his malformed and useless legs behind him, keeping pace with the procession. All were singing their hearts out with "joyful hope of the coming of our Savior Jesus Christ." Yes, it is possible, I now know, to shout for joy and exult in anticipation and belief.

The Gospel reading for today departs from the celebration and takes us to John the Baptist, who is speaking to crowds who have been following him, wanting to know what they can do to be baptized, for they surely want to be a part of John's promise that the road will be made straight and all flesh will see the salvation of God. What is this salvation of which all so eagerly want to be a part? Clearly and simply John answers their question, "What should we do?"

"Whoever has two cloaks should share with the person who has none; and whoever has food must do likewise." He exhorts the tax collector to not collect "more than the amount pre-scribed," and to soldiers he counsels, "Do not extort money from anyone by threats or false accusation." This, to prepare the way of the coming of the Savior—ancient platitudes from another culture? We need only to look at Wall Street, to look at our own country's war crimes, to look in our own cup-boards and closets. We need only look at our own growing lines of homeless people in soup kitchens and shelters, the mil-lions of uninsured in our country who need health care, the greed of those who misuse our land without regard to future generations. And to ponder our easy accusation of others. I look at my own bulging closets, my jammed-full cupboards, and at how easily accusations of others spring to my lips.

That night in Southern Sudan we all settled on stools or mats on the ground. A young couple proudly brought their newborn child to the altar, and they became our Holy Family. So close to what we awaited—a family truly in exile, as were

Mary, Joseph, and ultimately Jesus. We heard the Gospel read in different languages, to be heard by all the different tribes attending the Mass.

That night in Southern Sudan, under the brilliant starlit sky, I heard no rancor, no rantings or railings against those who have plenty. I heard no accusations against those of a different tribe. For a few short hours fear of the bombs dissolved.

We all just sat together in joyful hope.

Fourth Sunday of Advent

Fr. Eugene Toland, MM

Bolivia

Micah 5:2–5a; Luke 1:46b–55; Psalm 80:1–7; Hebrews 10:5–10; Luke 1:39–45 (46–55)

He has brought down the powerful from their thrones, and lifted up the lowly; he has filled the hungry with good things, and sent the rich away empty. —Luke 1:52–53

The readings today, like those of all the days of Advent, are proclamations of a hope grounded in the fact that God appeared in human flesh to become part of the problem that humans themselves create through blindness, selfishness, and greed.

Today's readings tell us to look for God working not through the great and powerful but through the small and those the great powers see as insignificant. "But you, Bethlehem-Ephrathah too small to be among the clans of Judah, from you shall come forth for me one who is to be ruler in Israel."

The rulers of the world take that message quite cynically with disbelief. But not those who believe, like Mary, who know that there is a deep-down, life-pulsing divine power within the mess, chaos, and self-destruction of our lives that calls us to create right relationships between ourselves and with creation all over again, time and time again, year after year. God is at work putting the divine dream into practice. That is why Mary did not listen to the cynics, the doubters when the news that Elizabeth was pregnant came. "In those days Mary set out and went with haste to a Judean town . . . where she entered the house of Zechariah and greeted Elizabeth." Mary believed, and then she hit the road to be with Elizabeth to celebrate that God is at work in what seems barren and hopeless to bring forth a new creation.

Bolivia is a country poor and exploited with a majority population that is indigenous. They are like the majority of people who live in the southern areas and who suffer the most from the destruction of the planet. Here in Bolivia those who believe are seeing that hand of God at work among their own people, and they are joining their hands and energies to restore God's dream of peace, reconciliation, and harmony with creation.

For centuries they were told that they did not matter, that progress would come from the north or Europe, from ideas forged in the civilization of the West. Those who were in control and even missioners told them that their way of seeing the world was "primitive," "quaint," "superstitious." Can anything good come from Bethlehem—or Bolivia?

Young Anabel Mamani sees thing differently. She is one of a new generation particularly of young women who take these readings today to heart. She represents a younger generation of Andean people who, motivated by both faith and an ancient cosmovision, take to the streets in joining organized groups to promote more sustainable use of Earth's resources by reducing consumption, by recycling, and by urging the governments to enact policies that protect and care for the land, water, and air for future generations. Anabel grew up with a reverence for Earth as mother—the Pachamama—whom her grandmother taught her to respect not as something apart from her but as intimately connected to her. So like other Andean people, she learned to tip a bit of whatever she drank to the ground "for Mother Earth" in thanksgiving for what Earth continues to give to humans. Such a view of life for Anabel blends easily with her Catholic faith in her worship of the God of life.

As it does for María Teresa, who insisted in her course of physical therapy that she would also spend time in the countryside to learn the ancient ways of healing from the elders, despite the cynical attitude of both her professors and fellow students. She now combines her studies of anthropology with the ancient understandings of her people. She says:

> God did not come to us with the Spanish misioners; God has always been with us, speaking through the good traditions and healing practices of our people. Israel was not the only vine that God was tending to. We also have prayed: "Restore us, O God of hosts; let your face shine, that we may be saved. Attend to this vine"—and God has heard us.

After centuries of exploitation by outsiders from Europe and the north and decades of neoliberal economic and political policies that only reinforced exclusion of the majority, some Catholics like Anabel and María Teresa are weaving together the ancient ways of relating to Earth. Inspiration from ancestors of their faith like Miriam and Mary give them hope and courage to begin from below to make a difference in how humans relate to one another and with Earth.

By such a commitment Anabel and María Teresa recognize that we are co-creators of God's creation, acting with hope and courage like Mary—one who believed.

Christmas Vigil (December 24)

Sr. Ann Braudis, MM

Bolivia and the Philippines

Isaiah 62:1–5; Psalm 89:4–5, 16–17, 27, 29;
Acts 13:16–17, 22–25; Matthew 1:1–25 or 1:18–25

Now the birth of Jesus the Messiah took place in this way. . . .
                                        —Matthew 1:18

May this Christmas Eve be full of blessings for all people and may peace resound all over the Earth!

This evening's Gospel speaks of the lineage of Jesus as it paints a picture of the whole of human history awaiting its Savior. Tonight, in a sense, we join the lineage of Jesus, one with Mary, one with Joseph, and one with David in anticipation and high hope. Indeed, we are one with the entire Cosmos as it trembles before the arrival of the Holy One of God. The very darkness of the night is full of expectation; the dawn lies just ahead.

In our hearts we know the meaning of Christmas:

♦ In the affection we feel for those we love
♦ In the willingness to forget grudges
♦ In the warm smiles and greeting we share with strangers
♦ In our hope for peace and abundance for all people
♦ And in our reaching out to those in need.

This Christmas Eve, across our planet, people will join together in a myriad of expressions of what tonight means. In a small village high in the Andes of Bolivia, the community will gather to reenact the first Christmas. They will compress the details of the story in order to have everything present in one beautiful celebration. In the cold mountain darkness they will follow a lighted star moved by a pulley across the village plaza; Mary will be there riding a donkey, Joseph by her side. The shepherds will follow along with the Magi. All will go into the small church and up to the sanctuary where the youngest baby of the village will become Jesus for the night. The other children will be angels singing the Christmas alleluia in their precious Quechua voices. Small crosses will be among the candles adorning the manger. By the door of the church, in the biting cold, they will drink hot cider. The night will be full of wonder, and its joy will sustain everyone for a long time to come.

In a mystical sense we too hold everything present tonight; sequential time is not important. We rejoice in the birth of a baby with minds running ahead to Jesus, the adult, who will call us to live a generous and noble life. Even as we remember what happened two thousand years ago, we are pulled to the future where hope resides and the promise of the fullness of life beckons. The daylight always hovers just ahead, and the chorus of angels forever announces a just and lasting peace.

May Jesus be born in you tonight as surely as he was born in Bethlehem all those long years ago.

May His promise be fulfilled in you, in those you love, and in the entire Earth community.

May the joy of this night sustain you for a long time to come.

Merry Christmas!

Christmas Mass at Midnight

Fr. Charlie Dittmeier, MM

Cambodia

Isaiah 9:1–6; Psalm 96:1–3, 11–13; Titus 2:11–14;
Luke 2:1–14

The people who walked in darkness have seen a great light.
                                                    —*Isaiah 9:2*

So many people walk in darkness in our world today. Some suffer from the darkness of war and conflict and natural disasters. Some experience the dark effects of economic turmoil. Some endure the darkness of repression and persecution or abuse. Some experience a darkness of disability or illness or depression. Others find darkness at work because of unfair practices; or maybe they have no job at all. Others endure the darkness of teasing or bullying or a lack of friends at school. Still others may feel a darkness within because of their inability to change patterns of sinfulness or hurtful behavior.

The deaf people of Cambodia are one group that has existed in a type of darkness. There were no deaf schools and no sign language in Cambodia before 1997. Effectively that means that there are no deaf adults in Cambodia today who have an education, who can read and write. Very few have even minimal sign language.

The Maryknoll Deaf Development Programme was set up to serve the deaf population of Cambodia. The first program it offers to young deaf adults—before job training, sign language interpreting, community development, social services—is basic education. Teachers give two years of nonformal education to these deaf youth who come to the program with no language and without ever having been to school one day in their life. The goal is to provide enough literacy and simple math and enough life skills that they will be able to support themselves and survive in a hearing world.

Early on, the teachers at the Deaf Development Programme noticed some strange dynamics in the classroom each time a new group of these young deaf people would start the program, something they couldn't quite put their finger on. Finally it dawned on the teachers what was happening. These young people—typically seventeen or eighteen to mid-twenties—were coming from isolated villages. They had never been to school and had no language at all. And the teachers came to realize that they didn't understand that the other students in the class with them were also deaf!

Up till that point, every time in their life they had been in a group of people they were the only deaf person in the group. They had never even met another deaf individual. They thought they were the only deaf person in the world. Actually they didn't even know what it means to be deaf, just that they were different from others in the village who would move their mouths while they didn't. Now in a classroom for the first time, they just assumed that all the other people there were hearing.

After helping them through that initial adjustment, the teachers teach sign language to these deaf youth as a first step, and it is amazing to see them come alive. From being isolated both geographically and linguistically, suddenly they have a group and a language and can communicate. For the first time, they have friends to talk to and to socialize with. After seeing all their younger brothers and sisters go off to school over the years, now they can go to school and wear a uniform, too. Independence beckons. The world opens to them. Life is good! It is gratifying to be part of a program that enables young people to discover who they are and what they can do and the life that is ahead of them.

"The people who walked in darkness have seen a great light." Jesus came to bring light and life to people, to all those who experience darkness in any form. Tonight we welcome and celebrate and thank God for this wonderful gift, this wonderful person who comes to us, who is God with us.

Jesus asks us to do the same, to bring light and life to others. On this Christmas Eve and through this Christmas season, it is easy to offer God's warmth and love to others. But as we welcome Jesus tonight, let us ask him to be our guide through all the coming year that we may help all God's people find their voice, true security, and just community as God's family of brothers and sisters.

Christmas Mass at Dawn

Sr. Charlotte Hobler, MM

Baltimore

Isaiah 62:11–12; Psalm 97:1, 6, 11–12; Titus 3:4–7; Luke 2:15–20

So they went with haste and found Mary and Joseph, and the child lying in the manger.   —*Luke 2:16*

Since February 2009, in a joint venture with two other Baltimore parishes, St. Vincent de Paul Church near the Inner Harbor has been hosting a lecture/discussion series on Elizabeth Johnson's *Quest for the Living God*. Attendees do their homework, and this makes for enthusiastic listeners and lively question/answer sessions. If you are familiar with this work you know its contents run the gamut from the mystery of God and the Trinity, through the contemporary face of evil and the emerging theologies, including liberation, feminist, black, Hispanic, and those that emerge from ecological worldviews.

I think of this group of Christians who try to make a genuine community within the oldest extant Catholic church building in Baltimore. I hear good things about their parish activities. I suspect no dilettantism among them, and their invitation to join the lecture series shows genuine interest in the mystery of God and humankind. If they wonder whether there are other redeemed worlds out there, their feet are still kept to the ground: witness the homeless who use the church's side lawn for bedding spots, clothing, and food supplies. That space is a refuge promised by pastor and community to be available until our city's mayor can provide shelter for all of Baltimore's homeless.

This juxtaposition of theological wonder among Christians along with the blessed poor neighbors makes for no surprise that this homily for Christmas Day is, in fact, being written in the heat of August. I wonder, if on the day this homily is published, world events will allow us space to ponder *kairos* (mystery) moments as well as *chronos* (reality) moments? What kinds of links will Christmas 2012 have to Isaiah and Psalm 97 and Titus and Luke: eternal words of hope that place us in mystery as real as our moments in regular time? Will we be able to hear with deep echoing thanks from the first lesson: "You shall be called, sought out, a city not forsaken?" and: "Light dawns for the righteous, and joy for the upright of heart" and "God our Savior . . . saved us, not because of any works of righteousness that we have done, but according to God's mercy . . ." that we might "become heirs according to the hope of eternal life." And what could move us more than Luke's mention of the mother of the child, who "pondered [these things] in her heart" as the neighbor shepherds saw what they saw with great joy, and felt included in this remarkable birthday party?

This day, as we recall the Incarnation, we can be overwhelmed. In his book *Engaged Spirituality*, Fr. Joseph Nangle, OFM, asks us to try to get our heads around "a completely Incarnate God":

> It's such a bold belief for humans. Because God's Incarnation is just that—an enfleshing of the Divine just the way all of humanity is enfleshed, through the natural process of conception, gestation, and birth . . . We hold that God in the person of Jesus was an embryo, a fetus, a newborn, an infant. He became a growing boy, an adult in formation; a relational human being; a friend, and yes, an enemy. He

died a horrible death and was buried in someone else's grave. He knew what to be human is. The concrete reality of the Incarnation is so amazing and far-reaching that it challenges our credence.

The book club will savor these thoughts.

So may the homeless poor at the Baltimore city church find God with them this day. May they find him in the guise of persons with food and clothes, and a spot to bed down. May they recognize themselves as "not forsaken," but cared for by other persons. Will they know what it is to be human when not everything is in graceful condition? City housing takes a very long time—and, a greater miracle yet, once they have more to share, will the homeless poor be moved to share among themselves? Will the respect shown to these shepherds bring them to fuller life as the day's liturgy brings them toward a noontime meal celebration of their brother's birthday?

Christmas Day Mass

Fr. Raymond Finch, MM

Cochabamba, Bolivia

Isaiah 52:7–10; Psalm 98:1–6; Hebrews 1:1–6;
John 1:1–18 or 1:1–5, 9–14

How beautiful upon the mountains are the feet of the messenger who announces peace, who brings good news, who announces salvation.   —Isaiah 52:7

Christmas is the celebration of new hope, of the good news that God is making the world anew. We live in a world where the bad news easily drowns out the Good News. Terrorism, war, corruption, greed, climate change, economic crisis, unemployment, racial and cultural conflict, interpersonal conflicts, broken families, and criminal violence are just a few of the threats that confront us each day. We truly need to hear Good News today, we need to be aware that God is present, in the midst of all these threatening realities; that God is with us struggling to bring about "a new heaven and a new earth." God is not way off in the sky or another dimension. God has pitched a tent among us: "And the Word became flesh and lived among us," and that changes everything.

In Bolivia it is common to hear that Christmas is for children. Individuals and organizations will go to incredible efforts to make sure each child, even the poorest, receives at least one toy, one present, and something special to eat or drink. During the days before Christmas there are endless lines of poor children in the towns and cities waiting for that toy, a cup of hot chocolate, and a piece of sweetbread. In the United States. we tell children about Santa Claus, who brings us what we want most; we take great joy and pleasure in the anticipation and delight of the children, even as we know who bankrolls Santa Claus. Do we think that Christmas is for children because we really don't believe, because we know that the toy and sweetbread will not reverse the undernourishment and poverty of so many children in Bolivia and other developing countries? Do we believe that Christmas is for children because deep down we know that we never receive our heart's desire? Are we so cynical as to say, "Let them enjoy it now before they find out the truth"? I think that we want to believe, but it is not easy to put everything at risk and act on the Good News in faith.

In Luke's version of the Christmas story Mary goes to visit Elizabeth, John the Baptist's mother, after saying yes to Gabriel's news that she will be the mother of Jesus. When Elizabeth heard Mary's greeting she responded, "Blessed are you among women, and blessed is the fruit of your womb. And why has this happened to me, that the mother of my Lord comes to me? For as soon as I heard the sound of your greeting, the child in my womb leaped for joy. "And blessed is she who believed that there would be a fulfillment of what was spoken to her by the Lord" (Luke 1:42–45). Mary had faith in God's promise. She heard the Good News, and she believed. She believed in God's saving presence even though she had no idea of how God would pull it off, even though she lived in a world torn apart by terrorism, war, corruption, greed, climate change, economic crisis, unemployment, racial and cultural conflict, interpersonal conflicts, broken families, and criminal violence. Despite all of her questions and doubts Mary said yes.

Hearing the Good News is important, believing in the powerful presence of God among us is critical, but it is all for naught if we do not act on what we have heard, if we do not live what we believe.

There is the story of a man who dreamed that God told him that he would win the Christmas lottery. He awoke very happy and began to anticipate all of the things that he could do with the money he would receive. One week passed, and then two weeks turned into months. Christmas was long gone. The man was disillusioned. Why would God fool him with that dream? That night he heard God again in a dream. He was angry and screamed: "You said that I would win the Christmas lottery. That was two months ago and here I am still broke, still without any money. Why did you trick me?" God answered: "You will win the lottery, this time it will not be the Christmas lottery, but you have to do your part, you have to get out there and buy a lottery ticket. Then you will win!" Am I doing my part?

This Christmas I pray that we have the openness to hear the Good News that God is among us, that God has pitched his tent in our midst, that God is bringing about a New Heaven and a New Earth. I pray that we might see God present in each newborn baby, in each child and in each person, even in the least among us. May we see and believe; may we have faith that God's promise is being fulfilled at this very moment even as we struggle with our questions and doubts. May we believe and may we act! May we do our part!

The Word was made flesh and dwells among us, and that makes all the difference! Merry Christmas!

Holy Family Sunday

Sr. Connie Krautkramer, MM

Tanzania

Sirach 3:2–6, 12–14; Psalm 128:1–5; Colossians 3:12–21;
Luke 2:41–52

*As God's chosen ones, holy and beloved, clothe yourselves with
compassion, kindness, humility, meekness, and patience.*
—*Colossians 3:12*

Today's feast of the Holy Family is an opportunity to think
about family: about who is family, about what it is that makes
a family holy, and about being members of God's family. In
our readings we heard how God desires an intimate relationship with us. God will bless us and keep us: "Let my face shine
upon you" (Numbers 6:25). God offers, like the warmth of
the sun on a chilly day. We heard the familiar story of shepherds visiting a new baby, born in one of their stables, and
how when he was eight days old the little boy was circumcised.
Joseph and Mary respected this religious law, yet Jesus grew
into a man who questioned the justice of many laws. Because
of him we are no longer slaves under the law, but free, and
responsible, to live as family, God's family.

Sometimes family means blood relatives, sometimes not.
There are laws that define who is family, and sometimes we
resort to DNA testing to help identify family. We speak of the
family of nations, and St. Francis extended family to include
all of creation.

God has a family; each one of us is a blessed daughter or son
of God. Do we believe all peoples of every nation are blessed
by God, or only our own? When we talk about God's blessings,

we often mention good health, or democracy, or freedom of speech and religion. Do we believe that we personally, or our nation particularly, deserve special blessings? And why would that be? Does God favor some children more than others?

A photograph on the front page of the *New York Times* on May 24, 2009, showed in stark detail the burial of a newborn baby. Wrapped in a colorful cloth, the baby lies at the bottom of a tiny newly dug grave. Women, their arms extended downward, circle the grave. Reading the article we learned that the photo was taken in Tanzania and that the infant died at birth because the mother did not have access to medical care for a complicated delivery.

I witnessed a similar situation in our neighborhood here in Tanzania. Out for a walk I came across women digging in the yard a short distance from their house. They told me a woman with severe malaria had lost her child, nearly full term, the night before. I wondered how God's face shines in such a situation. Is God looking into the hole? Is God mourning the loss of her child? Is God judging those who allow such tragedy to happen? Malaria kills children every day in Africa. Does that matter? Does everybody in the world have the right to basics like health care and clean water? Are these mothers, these infants, part of my family, after all? In God's eyes, yes!

Do I resent the needs of others when I fear there is not enough of something to go around, when I imagine there is a shortage and I might not get some of whatever it is? Or do I fear I might not get enough of it? How much is enough? I need to challenge myself when I think I am more entitled than my brothers and sisters who share the precious and limited resources of this Earth, and when I act as if laws should protect my rights and ignore those of others.

Our family is holy when we respect and trust one another, when we are willing to take time to listen well and to challenge each other. We are holy families when our hearts go out into the neighborhood, to the whole country and across boundaries to the entire world. We are holy when we recognize we do not have all the answers and that we need the ideas and perspectives of other members of God's family, all around the world.

May God's face shine upon us, each of us, all of us, God's entire family.

Feast of Mary, Mother of God (January 1)

Sr. Janice McLaughlin

Maryknoll, N.Y.

Micah 5:1–4; Psalm 80:2–3, 15–16, 18–19; Hebrews 10:5–10; Luke 1:39–45

When Elizabeth heard Mary's greeting, the child leaped in her womb. —*Luke 1:41*

The people of Zimbabwe, where I worked for more than thirty years, have many names for God. My favorite is Chipindikure—the One Who Turns Things Upside Down. It comes from the word, *kupinduka,* to be uprooted.

A young Jewish girl named Mary experienced this reality when an angel announced to her that she had been chosen to be God's mother. Imagine how this announcement upset her whole life. She would be uprooted from all she had known and the future she had imagined for herself. She said *yes* to being turned upside down. "Here I am, the servant of the Lord; let it be done to me according to your word." What an act of faith and love!

The angel told her that her cousin Elizabeth had also conceived through God's miraculous intervention and was six months into her pregnancy. Mary allows herself to be uprooted again as she rushes off to help Elizabeth in spite of her own situation. Luke tells us, "Mary set out and went with haste to a Judean town in the hill country." There were no comfortable cars, buses, or trains to take her there. Mary probably rode on the back of a donkey over the rocky countryside, setting aside her own worries to help another.

When she arrives and greets her cousin, Mary proclaims a magnificent hymn to God's transforming love. God raises the lowly and brings down the mighty, she says. God feeds the hungry and sends the rich away empty. God turns the values of this world upside down. This revolutionary message is the hallmark of our Christian faith.

In today's first reading, this option for the poor and the lowly is fulfilled in history. We are told that Bethlehem-Ephrathah, the smallest of the clans of Judah—will bring forth the ruler of Israel. His greatness shall reach "to the ends of the earth; and he shall be the one of peace." The contradiction between the world's vision of greatness and that of the Gospel is again made clear: the Gospel places value on peace rather than power.

The second reading from Hebrews reiterates God's desire for love and justice rather than for outward conformity to legal prescriptions such as sacrifice and burnt offerings. God again turns the values of the world upside down.

The beginning of a new year is traditionally a time to examine our lives. It is common for many people to look back over the past year to see what went well for them and to decide what changes they want to make. They also look forward to the coming year, with a fresh resolve to amend their lives for the better: to live with integrity and consistency. The new year then is a time to let God turn us upside down, a time to ask God to free us from what enslaves us and to embrace the uprooting that this might require. It is our time to say Yes to God.

Mary's "Yes" led her almost immediately to serve someone in need. Our Yes may also demand that we relinquish our own comfort to help our less fortunate brothers and sisters, wherever they may be.

Let us ask ourselves how we can be servants of God. What will this commitment require of us? What needs might we be asked to meet? What changes will we be expected to make? Mary's courage can inspire us. A teenage mother without a husband was frowned upon in Mary's day even more than in our own. And yet her great faith led her to announce: "All generations will call me blessed; for the Mighty One has done great things for me." Let us believe that God will do great things for us if we only say Yes.

Epiphany Sunday

Fr. Michael J. Snyder, MM

Tanzania

Isaiah 60:1–6; Psalm 72:1–7; Ephesians 3:1–12;
Matthew 2:1–12

*When they saw that the star had stopped they were overwhelmed
with joy.* —*Matthew 2:10*

On Epiphany, a joyous occasion for Christians throughout the
world, we conclude the Christmas season by remembering the
visit of the Magi, the three wise men from the East. They came
to Bethlehem, to the manger where the child lay.

I have lived in Tanzania, East Africa, for twenty-four years,
nineteen of those years spent among herding people in the
northeastern rural region. So I want you to think of the smells
of goats, sheep, and cattle in a muddy corral. Think of the
other creatures, the flies that must have been there. The Magi
were rich, educated, well-dressed men, coming to pay hom-
age. In the midst of it all they humbly prostrated themselves
on the ground in that stable and unfolded their gifts. What a
unique sight that must have been!

Ever since that first Epiphany, that first revelation to the
world of the newborn Messiah, each year believers throughout the world find hope in the story of these three men who
went on a journey with a vision: they were in search of something that gives true meaning to life, the search for truth. And
they believed that it might be realized in the fulfillment of the
prophecy found in the holy books of Israel: "Rise up in splendor, Jerusalem! Your light has come; the glory of the Lord
shines upon you. . . . See, darkness covers the earth, and thick

clouds cover the peoples; but upon you the Lord shines, and over you appears his glory. Nations shall walk by your light and kings by your radiance."

The three wise men found what they were looking for; they left the darkness and basked in the promised light. Their journey, their vision, and what they found in Bethlehem have been a source of faith and hope for all of us. But what has happened since that day? Why does it seem that throughout history in different places and among varied situations darkness continues to prevail? Why does the light seem dimmed for so many over these many generations?

In remembering the events of that Epiphany day, if we wish to answer these questions, then we need remember King Herod's role in the story. Remember, the Magi received a message in a dream not to return to Herod, so they went back to their own country by another route. Herod was driven by jealousy, that age-old concern for self over others that dates back to Adam and Eve. Even though his nation was, in fact, governed by Rome, his world vision remained restricted to maintaining the semblance of rule left to him. He couldn't see beyond himself, his little kingdom, and his minimal power. Each of us will need to reflect upon Herod and the Magi and then decide which path we will follow.

Looking at Africa and dating back to colonial times the preferential option has been for the Herod model. Colonial powers milked Africa of its mineral and human resources for personal and national gratification. Development for Africa was minimal. The legacy of slavery and colonialism has left deep scars upon Africa's cultures and its people. Independence came quickly to many nations in the early 1960s. When it did the European powers left just as fast; the new African leaders were not prepared.

Many look at Africa today and what they see is poverty, political instability, civil wars, genocide, drought, hunger, disease. Having lived here for these many years I experience some of these realities but what I witness is a people who are so strong in character; a people imbued with the hope that they can deal with the obstacles and achieve a better life; a people who revel in the joy of the Magi: a testimony to the meaning of faith.

Certainly political and economic policies on the world scene have had profound impacts upon development in Africa. Tanzania depends on aid from donor countries for nearly 40 percent of its national budget. This funding has been affected by the recent economic downturn. I serve as chaplain at the national medical university. Recently, the start of a new academic year was delayed one month because government-subsidized funding for students had not yet come through. As I prepared this homily, electricity had been cut fourteen hours for three of the last four days. They say it is largely due to the drought. But as I look over the reality I unfortunately see Herod alive and well in Tanzania: Corruption steeped in jealousy and greed has played a major part in the continued underdevelopment of Africa.

The rich are so rich and the masses so poor! The mining industry has grown in this country, but with little government control and less regard for the environment, surrounding rivers and soil have been poisoned. People have become sick and some have died. Now they are displaced from their traditional lands. Major profits from this industry are taken outside the country. The prime beneficiaries are expatriates and the nouveau riche of Tanzania. Where has the model of the Magi gone; where is that radiant light that brought us from darkness; where is the search for truth? Why do some continue to be filled with jealousy and greed? Why do they prefer Herod?

I say some because, in my experience, for the majority the light remains. It shines in the hearts of the multitude, the masses of people striving to cope with the struggles of the day, the poor among whom Jesus was born so many years ago. These are the ones whose zeal and joy for life prevail over the threatening conditions that surround them. They will not be denied the Epiphany, the revelation of God's presence among them in truth. And I believe that through their struggles the hearts of those who prefer Herod too will change. We can never cease to hope, for truth cannot be hidden, the light cannot be extinguished.

Then you shall be radiant at what you see, your heart shall throb and overflow, for riches of the sea shall be emptied out before you, the wealth of nations shall be brought to you. . . . All from Sheba shall come bearing gold and frankincense, and proclaiming the praises of the LORD!

Baptism of the Lord

Phil Dahl-Bredine, former Maryknoll lay missioner

Mexico

Isaiah 42:1–4, 6–7; Psalm 29:1–4, 3, 9–10; Acts 10:34–38;
Luke 3:15–16, 21–22

*"I baptize you with water; but one who is more powerful than I
is coming."* —*Luke 3:16*

Shortly after his baptism in the River Jordan we find Jesus in
Nazareth proclaiming in no uncertain terms what the three
short years of his earthly mission will be about: *He has anointed
me to bring good news to the poor. He has sent me to proclaim
release to the captives and to give recovery of sight to the blind, to
let the oppressed go free, to proclaim the year of the Lord's favor.*

Jesus did not invent this description of his calling. He
found it in the deep scriptural tradition of the Jewish Torah
as recalled in our first reading today. His announcement in
Nazareth unpacks the concept of "justice" that God's servant
in Isaiah will bring to the nations. It is a justice that, in Peter's
words, shows no partiality. It is for all nations of the human
family.

In the same way that Jesus' baptism by John was part of
the process through which he clarified his calling, our baptism
could help us to recognize that we, the family of his followers,
also have Jesus' same calling.

Yet, to be honest, we need to ask, "Where is good news
being brought to the poor in our day? Who is proclaiming
release to captives and freeing the oppressed? "The year of
the Lord's favor" in Hebrew scripture represents the Jewish
jubilee year when slaves are freed and wealth is redistributed

equitably in the community. Who is announcing that redistribution today?

Unfortunately, we probably need to admit that neither our country nor our church is much involved in carrying out this mission that Jesus describes. Where then do we look for the prophetic voices and the prophetic activists who are bringing good news to the poor, freeing the oppressed, and declaring economic redistribution?

It seems that God continues to show no partiality in regard to the nations or faiths from which he chooses his prophets. For some of the strongest voices that ring like good news in the ears of the poor, the most reasonable voices for lifting centuries of oppression of people of color in the Americas, and the most insistent voices for a just economic redistribution come today from the global South.

The voices of the indigenous peoples of Mexico, Ecuador, and Bolivia are strong and clear. Evo Morales, indigenous president of Bolivia, declares in his ten commandments for saving humanity and the planet:

- ◆ We must develop relations of coexistence and not oppression of one country by another, without imperialism and without colonialism.
- ◆ Basic services such as water, electricity, education, health, and collective transportation should be recognized as human rights.
- ◆ We must consume only what is necessary, carefully prioritize what we produce, consume local products and do away with consumerism, waste, and luxury. It is not understandable that some families seek only luxury while millions of people do not have the possibility of living well.

Similarly, at the first forum against the Plan Puebla Panama in Tapachula, Mexico, in 2002, Mexican indigenous campesinos declared prophetically: The earth and water, the forests, biodiversity, agricultural knowledge, traditional medicine, and the indigenous culture are communal goods, part of the common patrimony of human beings, and are not merchandise.

Does this remind us of Jesus' anger at seeing the money changers turning the things of God into commerce? Or have we who claim to be his followers lost his just anger, his commitment to freedom from oppression for all, his commitment to a just distribution of the goods of creation? Can God depend on us to once again take up the prophetic role along with the other prophetic voices we find in our human family today to do what is right for our human family and the planet?

Theologian Ched Myers calls for us to recognize the "Great Economy" that God has been trying to communicate to us through the centuries, the Great Economy of those who believe that creation has provided abundance for us all if we learn—as the Israelites had to learn in the desert and as Jesus tried to convince us—to take only what we need from this beautiful planet. That Great Economy insists on the right of everyone to share at the table of God's generosity.

Good news for the poor, freedom for the oppressed, the year of economic favor—that is our baptismal calling.

Second Sunday in Ordinary Time

Sr. Mary Ann Smith, MM

Washington, D.C., and the Philippines

Isaiah 62:1–5; Psalm 96:1–3, 7–10;
First Corinthians 12:4–11; John 2:1–12

Now there are varieties of gifts, but the same Spirit; and there are varieties of services, but the same Lord.
—1 Corinthians 12:4–5

Today's readings speak of God's love for all of creation and desire for a society founded on justice. In Psalm 96 all creation rejoices in the splendor and beauty of the universe. We are called to care for creation and work for the common good of our neighbors. The diverse gifts of the Spirit (1 Corinthians 12:4–11) are available to each of us to use according to our own talents in whatever situations we find ourselves. In our day the Spirit is leading us towards building a world of peace with justice and the integrity of creation.

As a missionary I have been privileged to meet many people in Africa, Asia, the Caribbean, South America, and the United States. The varieties of cultures and individual gifts I have encountered have enriched my life and are a powerful witness to the beauty, majesty, and diversity of creation and, especially, the goodness in all people. I have met many women and men who, often at great sacrifice to themselves and their families, choose to work to improve the lives of their neighbors and local communities.

In Baguio City, Philippines, young men and women worked on the staff or as volunteers in our adult education program to encourage indigenous people in the area to participate in literacy and community organization programs. The learning exchange between the adult and youth learners demonstrated a variety of gifts and showed that formal education is not the only form of education. While the adults were illiterate, they were extremely intelligent and competent people.

Nena, one of the literacy learners, was one of the most intelligent people I have ever met. She was recognized as the leader in her community and used her gifts to encourage others to attend literacy classes and community organization meetings. People like Nena all over the world motivate family, neighbors, and friends to take often difficult steps to improve the quality of their lives. On the other hand, the challenge and opportunity offered to the youth in this program have influenced their life choices and the way they look at people who may be different from them.

In Honduras, Elias, an agriculturalist, was committed to protecting the national environment. His knowledge and expertise with regard to the soils, plants, and animals in the various ecosystems were essential to improving both the ecosystems and the lives of poor people. Elias could not walk into a field without getting down on his knees, picking up a handful of soil, and explaining whether it was good or not. He was always happy to assist local communities and teach them how to protect their soils and water while increasing their harvests.

One of the overarching principles in sharing the gifts of the Spirit is commitment to community and the common good. In the Gospel (John 2:1–12) the familiar story of the wedding feast at Cana is a community story. Jesus and his disciples were invited to the wedding. He was among friends and family. His mother was close enough to the bridegroom that she wanted to prevent him from being embarrassed on his wedding day. Mary did not ask Jesus to work a miracle. It seems Jesus was not thinking of beginning his ministry right there and then. But he responds to the movement of the Spirit prodded by his mother's concern and works his first miracle in a community context. The Spirit continues to blow where it will today in our church and society. It is our challenge to respond to today's needs and use our gifts and talents to work for peace with justice and the integrity of creation.

Third Sunday in Ordinary Time

Fr. Steve Judd, MM

Bolivia

Nehemiah 8:2–4a, 5–6, 8–10; Psalm 19: 8, 9, 10, 15;
First Corinthians 12:14–30; Luke 1:1–4; 4:14–21

The Spirit of the Lord is upon me, because he has anointed me to bring good news to the poor.   —*Luke 4:18*

The Small Christian Community to which I belong and where I am blessed to serve as a sacramental minister in the city of Cochabamba, Bolivia, proudly carries the name of the Spanish Jesuit priest Luis Espinal, who was martyred on March 22, 1980. His death occurred two days before that of El Salvador's better-known and universally revered Archbishop Oscar Romero. Espinal's death has often been overlooked except by those of us in Bolivia who cherish the memory of his extraordinary witness amid the circumstances of the time under a brutal military dictatorship. Yet the thirty-third anniversaries of the martyrdom of Romero, Espinal, and the four U.S. churchwomen, murdered December 2, 1980, in El Salvador, along with thousands of other contemporary martyrs that the Latin American church will celebrate this year, all serve to keep alive the "dangerous memory" of a church committed to the poor and those who seek justice and human dignity.

Barely out of his teenage years, Espinal arrived in Bolivia as a young Jesuit scholastic in the late 1960s and quickly immersed himself in the life and struggles of his newly adopted land, taking up the cause of the indigenous young people in La Paz through his ministries in social communications. His weekly radio messages, creative work in cinema, and written essays earned him a large following and emboldened him to speak truth to power at great personal risk.

The small book of prayers he published, *Oraciones a quema-ropa* (Prayers at close range), constitute an incisive critique of the dictatorial regime at that time along with insights into the consequences of discipleship, of discerning the pattern of his life in following the life and ministry of Jesus in such a conflictive context. One prayer in particular speaks of ceasing to be Christians in a "routine" and ordinary way. Another holds up the example of Jesus as one who didn't act "prudently" in the face of injustices. Espinal was one of the first to see that a mere passport did not exempt the missioner from the fate and destiny of the people who claimed him as one of their own.

Like for so many others committed to the cause of justice in Latin America, today's familiar Gospel reading (Luke 4:16–21) became the foundational biblical text for Espinal. Found only in Luke's Gospel and based on the words of the prophet Isaiah (61:1–3), the stirring words that Jesus proclaims in the synagogue of his hometown of Nazareth capture the imagination, the essence, and the journey of those living and working in Latin America and around the world whose lives have been transformed by the "physical and spiritual nearness to the poor," in the words of the Peruvian theologian Gustavo Gutiérrez.

Recent biblical scholarship and research have greatly enhanced our understanding of this richly evocative text to underscore even more its significance as the spiritual foundation for missionary discipleship. The text has its origins in the Hebrew practice of the Sabbatical and Jubilee years when debt forgiveness and release of the slaves were mandated. When Jesus quotes the words of Isaiah, "to proclaim the year of the Lord's favor" (verse 21), he makes a clear reference to a

Jubilee year. In fact, one can make a strong and compelling case for reading all of the Lucan writings in the perspective of the Sabbatical–Jubilee tradition. This year of the "C" cycle of readings focused on the Gospel of Luke provides us with a unique opportunity to reread the Gospel in the Sabbatical Year–Jubilee key.

Similarly, the Nehemiah text (8:2–4a, 5–6, 8–10) from the first reading comes out of the same Sabbatical Year–Jubilee tradition but is situated in the time of a return of the Jewish people from the trauma of the Babylonian Exile. The long-awaited restoration to the Promised Land is one of those graced moments on which to rebuild the dispersed community, a *kairos* experience of a renewal of God's covenant with the people of Israel. The spirit of the Pauline second reading from 1 Corinthians presents a vision of the kind of ideal community we seek to build with all of its diverse and complementary gifts and ministries. Created in the image of the Body of Christ this vision will carry forward the mission of Jesus in whatever sociocultural context it occurs.

With the memory of the anniversaries of Espinal, Romero, Maura, Ita, Jean, and Dorothy ever present in our hearts and minds, we can all celebrate with communities around the world a Jubilee Year mindful that we all are called to stand up in the synagogue and before the assemblies of our churches and congregations to proclaim a "year of the Lord." For truly we have been blessed to dwell among witnesses like these and countless others whose lives are patterned on that of Jesus. When our small community in Cochabamba pauses to celebrate the memory of Luis Espinal on March 22, we will discover anew our own calls and commitment to missionary discipleship in a graced historical moment.

Fourth Sunday in Ordinary Time

Sr. Teresa Dagdag, MM

Philippines

Jeremiah 1:4–5, 17–19; Psalm 71:1–6, 15–17;
First Corinthians 12:31–13:13 or 13:4–13; Luke 4:21–30

They will fight against you; but they shall not prevail against you, for I am with you, says the LORD, *to deliver you.*
—*Jeremiah 1:19*

In the first reading, Jeremiah warns the people of Judah of the impending doom that is about to befall the southern kingdom. The Babylonians would invade Judah, resulting in loss of land; the burning of the Holy City, Jerusalem; and the devastation of the Temple in 587 B.C.E. as well as the deportation of Judah's king to Babylon. Without a king, land, or Temple, Judah would have no future; the people that was once holy and faithful has become estranged from God. Walter Brueggemann calls Jeremiah's prophetic message a "classic indictment, asserting that Israel has forfeited the relationship with Yahweh." The people of Judah did not heed Jeremiah's prophetic message. It was only after the destruction of the Temple that the captured peoples in exile reflected on their experience of disaster. The reflection arose from the community that restored hope in God's promise to write the law on their hearts; God will make a new covenant with God's people (Jeremiah 31:33).

Like the destruction of the Temple, the devastation of the environment shocks us. Forests are decimated, rivers are polluted, mines and other natural resources are exploited in such massive proportions that so often render them depleted, and innumerable species become extinct. The world that we know today has been characterized by the effects of climate change—typhoons are becoming stronger and changes in weather patterns are happening. We have been warned that if we continue with the massive destruction that we inflict on Earth, our children will have no future.

My mission experience was in the Philippines, where the rapid disappearance of the forest cover has caused flash floods. Logs have been exported to colonial economic centers that preserve their own forests at the expense of developing countries. Typhoons in September–October 2009 resulted in more than one thousand deaths in Luzon. Metropolitan Manila was 80 percent flooded; thousands living along Laguna de Bay were rendered homeless; more than five hundred people in the Cordillera bioregion perished in landslides, which also claimed houses, livelihoods, roads, and bridges. Human practices constitute a major cause of the devastation: the loss of forest cover; the deteriorating vigilance of residents along floodways; the lack of inadequate spillways to drain river water into the ocean; mindless solid waste management causing blockage of drainage systems. We have been negligent in protecting the environment.

Reflecting on these recent calamities juxtaposed with the Temple's destruction in the sixth century B.C.E., we learn valuable lessons. Just as the community in Judah and those deported to Babylon reflected on the destruction of the Temple, we too reflect on the environmental destruction around us. Numerous warnings from indigenous and international prophets about the disastrous future of Planet Earth remain unheeded. Loss of lives and livelihood and the plight of ecological refugees prompt us to reflect on our failure to develop a nurturing relationship with the environment. The God who appointed Jeremiah also calls us "to build and to plant." Let me offer three points:

1. Building community during calamities. Community building is anchored in the kind of love described in today's second reading. Calamities have a way of building a sense of community. Countless acts of heroic bravery and neighborliness were witnessed in flooded and landslide sites. Neighbors helped one another; people donated relief goods, and volunteers packed and delivered them to needy victims facilitated by churches, TV stations, and government agencies. An eighteen-year-old construction worker, a good swimmer, risked his life to save thirty people. He then heard a distressed call from a helpless mother to save her baby, which he did. Calamities have a way of evoking love that is kind and patient, that bears all things and endures all things for others.

2. Innovative response to devastation. Devastation has a way of inspiring a positive response from people. One example was the people's response to their experience of loss due to landslides in Atok, Benguet, which destroyed fifty houses and farms. The devastation prompted the community leaders to think of planting a hundred thousand trees that would mitigate future occurrences of flooding and landslides. The plan by women leaders is to set up a seedling program to reforest their balding mountainous region. Innovative response to Earth's need for rehabilitation emerged as a result of the devastation. These leaders manifest the Psalmist's response: "You who have made me see many troubles and calamities will revive me again; from the depths of the earth, you will bring me up again" (Psalm 71:20–21).

3. Universal response to climate change. A universal response is urgently needed to address climate change today. The call is for the Earth community, human and other-than-human,

to go beyond national boundaries. Among other means, the human species could develop alternative low-carbon lifestyles, reduce energy consumption, improve its efficiency, and use renewable sources of energy. In the Gospel reading, Jesus says that the Spirit of the Lord sent him "to proclaim the year of the Lord's favor." This means to celebrate the jubilee for the land, to celebrate the jubilee for the Earth. Observing jubilee is observing God's statutes to "faithfully keep my ordinances, so that you may live on the land securely. The land will yield its fruit and you will eat your fill and live on it securely" (Leviticus 25:18). In asserting his mission, however, Jesus was questioned for being merely Joseph's son. When he reasoned that he was sent to fulfill a universal mission, Jesus was driven out of town and was almost hurled off a cliff. We know that Jesus' strong commitment to build the Kingdom of God led him to his passion and death.

Jeremiah offered a word of hope performed through his life and the choices he made. God's final word is not destruction and annihilation; it is restoration and reunion: reunion with God, reunion with one another, reunion with the land, reunion with the Earth community. God's call is for us to restore a caring relationship with creation. We are called to a universal mission to nurture Earth, echoing Pope Benedict XVI's World Peace Day message in 2010: "If you want to cultivate peace, protect creation." The call for universal solidarity invokes intergenerational responsibility for the future. The pope calls on all to be "responsible for the protection of the environment. This responsibility knows no boundaries" (no. 11). Protecting the natural environment in order to build a world of peace is thus a duty incumbent upon each and all (no. 14).

Fifth Sunday in Ordinary Time

Tim O'Connell, former Maryknoll lay missioner

El Salvador

Isaiah 6:1–2, 3–8; Psalm 138:1–5, 7–8; First Corinthians 15:1–11 or 15:3–8, 11; Luke 5:1–11

When they had brought their boats to shore, they left everything and followed him.   *—Luke 5:11*

Like most people, when I was a teenager, I was unsure of what I wanted to do in the future. I only knew that I wanted to serve others and be part of something larger than myself. I looked for someone to emulate among the people I knew. I admired my grandfather, who enlisted to fight in World War I at age seventeen. Decades later, as a husband and father, he reenlisted to fight fascism in World War II. My father and uncles always talked about their dad's commitment to country and followed in his footsteps. Through these men, the military became my model of service, so at age seventeen, I enlisted.

It didn't occur to me that by signing that contract, I made myself available to military and political leaders to pursue what they determined to be the vital national interests. I didn't think about what this might mean for me as a Catholic, nor was I challenged by anyone, including my church, to do so.

The readings today do challenge us to think about what it means to follow Jesus. This is no easy task. Sometimes we do it well; sometimes we don't. We doubt God, and we sin. The readings make this clear, but they also offer hope, revealing God intimately involved in the human experience. Despite our imperfections, we can find healing, forgiveness, and love in God.

The readings express a sense of gratitude for this involvement of the Creator in our lives. So much so, that in the reading from Isaiah when the Lord asks, "Whom shall I send?" The response is unequivocal: "Send me." As much as today's readings are about sin and forgiveness, doubt and faith, they are also about answering God's call.

But what does that look like in our daily lives? I suppose it means something different for everyone, as God has granted us each different gifts.

But authentically following Jesus would include a life filled with solidarity, compassion, and love. I'm reminded of the motto of the Jesuit Volunteer Corps: "Ruined for life." These volunteers, Maryknoll missioners, and too few others leave behind the lives they know to be witnesses to the Gospel and to encounter God in other people. They are forever transformed.

Why might such people consider themselves "ruined"? Could it be that in meeting the "other" we learn something about our common humanity? We come to see ourselves, and Christ, in the coffee picker in El Salvador and the teenager renting her body in Cambodia. We realize that we're vulnerable and that our well-being is inextricably connected to that of our sisters and brothers in dusty villages and crowded slums around the world. We learn that security, be it national or financial, is illusory. It's an idol distracting us from God and our true mission of Love. To be "ruined" is to be resurrected into new life, conscious of our weaknesses but confident in God's companionship. It is to live counter to the prevailing culture of unthinking consumerism and glorified violence.

People following Jesus exude joy amid the suffering that is part of being human. They are deliberate in using precious resources to feed the hungry, clothe the naked, and house the homeless. They work to build civil society instead of violently suppressing civil unrest. They use their imaginations to create life-sustaining solutions rather than devising the means of our destruction. And they do all this with love.

Consider what the world would be like if following Jesus were the norm? Imagine if more people addressed the root causes of poverty and injustice than joined the military. Imagine the Agency for International Development with the funding and personnel of the Pentagon—and vice versa. Imagine converting the military industrial complex into a peace and prosperity nexus.

Most people will say, "That's impractical," "That's impossible," or "We've tried and it doesn't work." Or as Simon Peter says in today's Gospel, "We have worked all night long but have caught nothing." He doubts Jesus but finds the faith to follow his command and lowers his nets. When he pulls them up and his boat fills with fish, he is filled with awe and drops to his knees. He is "ruined."

With this act Jesus is saying, "I will make you builders of the common good and promoters of peace. In me, everything is possible."

Today's readings invite us to join Jesus in his mission of love, peace, justice, and joy. Our call is to leave everything, follow, and be all that we can be!

Ash Wednesday

Sr. Bibiana Bunuan, MM

Namibia

Joel 2:12–18; Psalm 51:3–6, 12–14, 17;
Second Corinthians 5:20–6:2; Matthew 6:1–6, 16–18

So we are ambassadors for Christ, since God is making his appeal through us; we entreat you on behalf of Christ, be reconciled to God. —*2 Corinthians 5:20*

Just beyond today's first reading, Yahweh answers the cry of the people: "The Lord was stirred to concern for his land and took pity on his people. [He said]: 'See, I will send you grain, and wine, and oil, and you shall be filled with them. No more will I make you a reproach among the nations." No longer will others doubt the goodness and mercy of God.

Yahweh desires fruitfulness, just and full development for people. In the past century, Namibians, whose country was part of South Africa until 1990, experienced a painful and violent history of apartheid. A policy of separate development made most people second-class citizens in their own homeland. Physical, social, psychological, and emotional violence left some with deep wounds that still make it difficult for them to move on with their lives. Dreams were shattered, and many lives were lost. A concrete example was the Bantu education system, in which black children were provided schooling inferior to white children. But black people fought for self-determination and ridded South Africa of oppressive laws that separated them from one another. In addition to battling oppressive laws, from 1966 to 1988 Namibia fought a war against the apartheid-era government of South Africa for its own independence.

The PEACE Center in Namibia has as its mission "to understand, assess, and address the dynamics of violence and trauma as well as the impact of violence and trauma on people's lives in Namibia and to effect healing and transformation." To make this mission concrete, one of its many programs, called the WEAT ("We are together") project, incorporates an Alternatives to Violence Program (AVP), with "healing of memories" and psychosocial support groups. This project seeks to reduce and ultimately prevent violence in Namibia. WEAT seeks to stop the cycle of violence within the victims, thus preventing victims from becoming perpetrators. The core value of AVP is transforming power—the power within oneself to creatively follow the path of nonviolence before a situation escalates. Healing of memories is a process of therapy as one confronts one's own violent memories and hears about those of others; telling one's own stories is a critical part of the healing process. The energy in these activities may create a space that someday leads to a truth and reconciliation commission to heal the nation for a lasting peace.

Vicky Festus, a nurse at the Center, can say by heart the words of the psalm: "Create in me a clean heart." With a compassionate heart, she knows the pain other freedom fighters felt during the war to liberate the country from the South African government. She herself was suspected of being a spy. She was imprisoned for two years in a dungeon along with her one-year-old son, leaving a three-year-old daughter on her own. Eventually reunited, she now has to heal her own and her children's wounds of abandonment.

Another kindhearted woman, Ame Bridgens, was not incarcerated with other freedom fighters but nonetheless was very active in "making the land for Yahweh" safe, just, and respectful for the peoples of Namibia. She worked with the Council of Churches of Namibia and with the late Bishop Hausiku to form the Justice and Peace Commission during the apartheid years. They kept people informed, had discussion groups, and undertook positive actions. Although the Commission dissolved after independence in 1990, Ame still fasts as she asks God to show her what direction is needed for reconciliation. She believes that "your Father who sees what is kept secret will reward you." Working with her now in the parish Justice and Peace Commissions makes me appreciate what people have endured to be free.

It is a privilege to work with Vicky and Ame. They convince me of how strong and resilient the human spirit can be. God alone knows people's hearts and will heal their wounds. They are truly ambassadors of peace and reconciliation in themselves, in their families, in the community, and in the whole nation.

First Sunday of Lent

Sr. Helene O'Sullivan, MM

Cambodia

Deuteronomy 26:4–10; Psalm 91:1–2, 10–15; Romans 10:8–13;
Luke 4:1–13

*When the Egyptians treated us harshly and afflicted us, by
imposing hard labor on us, we cried to the* LORD, *the God of our
ancestors; the* LORD *heard our voice and saw our affliction, our
toil and our oppression.* —*Deuteronomy 26:6–7*

On this first Sunday in Lent, the first reading tells the story
of the people who are suffering under the yoke of slavery
imposed by the powerful Egyptian empire. In their misery,
they call out to Yahweh for deliverance. God hears their cries
and brings them out of slavery and suffering into a land flowing with milk and honey.

The women and children who have come to the shelter
where I work in Cambodia have also escaped what Pope John
Paul II called a modern-day form of slavery: human traffick-
ing in the sex trade. Some of the women and their children
have escaped the misery of domestic violence, and younger
girls have escaped the violence of rape. For them, the shelter
is a land flowing with milk and honey, a place of kindness and
safety where their need for food, rest, and medical care are
provided for by caring people.

Over the years, I have seen that the women and girls who
enter the shelter from backgrounds of grinding rural poverty
carry expectations about life that emerge from a sense of sufficiency. Earth yields what it can to provide for our needs and
it is enough, it is sufficient. We in turn care for Earth and take

no more from it than it can replenish, re-grow and renew. The mutuality in their relationship with Earth and their environment is a source of inspiration to me since I come from New York City. Caring for Earth and its resources is something I had to learn while living in harmony with the environment—without waste and without excess—while the sixty or more women and children in the shelter live this relationship from birth.

When the torrential rains come, water is collected by gutter pipes on the edge of the roof and directed into huge earthen jars that are four feet high and four feet wide with a broad opening from which the women draw the water that they pour over themselves to bathe and wash their clothes. A group of the women or girls will wrap sarongs around themselves and stand around the two large jars scooping out water and chatting. They usually bathe together at noon when the sun heats up the water a bit. The smaller children are thrilled when they are finally tall enough to be able to scoop pan-fulls of water out of the large earthen jars by themselves.

There are no refrigerators in the shelter as food is bought fresh from the market for that day and wrapped in newspaper. There is no plastic packaging to dispose of. After all have eaten their fill, some of the leftovers are left out for the cats that are busy keeping down the rat population. The rest is put in a bucket to be collected in the evening by a local farmer to feed to his pigs. Dishes are washed and put on racks to dry in the sun, eliminating the need for towels, which saves time, water, soap, and finding a place big enough to hang them to dry.

Small children in Cambodian villages and even the streets of Phnom Penh wear oversized T-shirts and no diapers. When they have an accident, their mothers take them over to the big jars where they are washed in scoopfuls of water and allowed to air dry! They never get diaper rash. (When the children leave the shelter to go to the doctor's office or to a court appearance with their mothers they do wear diapers.)

Each woman sleeps with all her children on a typical Cambodian slatted wooden bed covered only with a woven mat. The mats are washed regularly, dry quickly, and last forever.

Most of the women and girls at the shelter have little or no education; while at the shelter they study a vocational skill, like sewing, so that they can support themselves and their families when they leave. They learn to use a pedal-driven machine, which does not need electricity; this is helpful when they return to the rural areas and even at the shelter as sometimes the electricity goes off for three or four hours during the day and again in the evenings.

One of my biggest challenges is not to complain—well, not too much anyway—especially when the electricity goes off and the fans stop working, forcing me to go outside peacefully and find some shade to continue pursuing some useful endeavor. Learning to go with the flow and rhythm of life is one lesson I still need to learn. If the electricity goes out I need to just let go of my self-imposed deadline and know that all will be fine. The work will get done in Cambodian time, not U.S. time.

When I try to go with the flow and follow the rhythms of nature I slow down enough to notice the beauty of a flower or to be struck again and again by the gorgeous faces and delightful smiles of Cambodia's children. In a shelter where there is sufficiency, I experience abundance, and I think the women and girls do too. I am grateful to God to be a part of this small oasis of "milk and honey" for these women and girls escaping such misery.

When I was home in the States one summer to visit my family and the Maryknoll Sisters Center, I was so inspired to see the emphasis on the environment and on the practical ways that people have found to save our planet. There is also a new spirituality growing along with this that is more inclusive of diversity and more respectful of life in all its forms. This spirituality sees the unity of all things and sees Earth and all its people as one. This spirituality reverences and recognizes the abundance we have already been given by our Creator. Recognizing this abundance in our midst is the key to letting go of the grasping so that all on our shared planet will have enough.

Second Sunday of Lent

Fr. Thomas Henehan, MM

Bolivia

Genesis 15:5–12, 17–18; Psalm 27:1, 7–9, 13–14;
Philippians 3:17–4:1 or 3:20–4:1; Luke 9:28–36

And while he was praying, the appearance of his face changed, and his clothes became dazzling white.   —Luke 9:29

Throughout Bolivia the complex global crisis (i.e., global warming, financial instability, growing gap between the rich and the poor, lack of intercultural dialogue, and the increase of violence) is seen as failing to understand the true meaning of life. Bolivians, on all levels, have struggled these past few years to articulate the true meaning of life and to incorporate it into the text of the national constitution that was approved by a referendum during 2009. They are looking for a radical change in understanding themselves as a nation. They are looking for ways to address the crisis daily lived out in Bolivia, South America's poorest country. They believe that the solution is intimately related to their very identity as a nation.

Bolivia has deep roots in the indigenous cultures that are the basic ingredients of the local identity. The attempt to turn things around and develop a new way of thinking (metaphysics) has found possible solutions in the cultures that make up their identity. For example, the Quechua word *Chakana* or the Aymará word *Jakaña* communicate an integral way to live and to perceive life.

These concepts highlight the difference between "living well" and "living better." The former is seen as opposed to the latter. "Living well" is understood as an integral concept that goes well beyond just existing. It is understood as all that is required to "live well": a household, relationships, respect, energy, audacity, beauty, and peace. It requires a spirit of receiving and being received. It implies a family spirit that cares for and nourishes a life of peace and enjoyment.

According to the Bolivian thinking, "living better" is the attitude that currently generates the multifaceted global crisis. In Bolivia it has resulted, among other evils, in causing many children to be orphans and elderly to be abandoned. They have realized that to live better than others—with its imposed rules and norms—ends up happening at the expense of others.

Although Bolivia is a long way from being a model to the planet of a people who have found the answer to the world's problems, with its indigenous tradition it has a great deal to contribute to a new way of thought and behavior.

In the readings of today's liturgy we find many elements that help us understand the need to recover our identity and identify the depth that is called forth in order to address current global challenges.

Today's readings speak of two key events: exodus and transfiguration.

Some authors maintain that the Transfiguration was an "exodus experience" for Jesus. An exodus, from this perspective, means leaving one reality or one way of behaving, and entering into a new stage of life and a new way of behaving, thereby becoming a crossroads moment in the life of Jesus.

The Transfiguration of Jesus can be understood as an internal and personal experience quite possibly during a time of prayer. It was a profound mystical prophetic experience. It was a way of being in touch with his own identity: he was not Moses and he was not Elijah as many had thought. As he stood between the two, the Father recognized him as his beloved son, his chosen one, and we are called to "listen to him!" That was important for Jesus as he was about to enter Jerusalem and face his passion and death, the initial event of a personal exodus that would culminate with the resurrection. The deepest part of Jesus was called forth by this exodus experience. Knowing of the love of his Father was what transfigured Jesus.

To experience this profound mystical experience, Jesus chose the three key leaders of what would become the early church: Peter, James, and John. Throughout their relationship with Jesus they had often been confused and disoriented. Peter is seen here as speaking out in favor of settling into a comfortable mode, looking for an easy way to avoid continuing on the road that would lead to the passion and death of Jesus, thus avoiding the real objective of the exodus, which is a new eternal reality, that is, life in all its fullness, "living well."

This Sunday's readings invite us to fully enter into a mystical prophetic experience with Jesus, not only relating to him as our Lord and Savior, but listening to him, following his teachings and imitating his life, his behavior, his way of relating to others, especially the excluded and the poorest of the poor. Just as Jesus grows in his identity as the Beloved, we are challenged to search within the deepest part of our lives and acknowledge our very identity as citizens and disciples of the Reign of God. The Transfiguration invites us to experience the love of the Father as Jesus did and to also be transfigured. It is only then that we will be able to meet the challenges of the current global crisis, opting not to "live better" but to "live well."

The Bolivian people are currently looking at what is being called forth from their rich tradition and indigenous cultures to generate a commitment to a mystical and prophetic way of life consistent with the orientation given in today's readings. How are we called forth from our rich tradition and culture to respond to today's global crisis?

How do we allow ourselves to be transfigured as disciples and missioners by the mystical and prophetic experience of the transfiguration of Jesus?

How can we be a sign to the world and faithful citizens of the Reign of God without being content like Peter with "being good that we are here"?

Third Sunday of Lent

Sr. Teresa Hougnon, MM

Maryknoll Sisters Peace Team, Nairobi, Kenya

Exodus 3:1–8, 13–15; Psalm 103:1–4, 6–8, 11;
First Corinthians 10:1–6, 10–12; Luke 13:1–9

*Then the LORD said, "I have observed the misery of my people
who are in Egypt; I have heard their cry on account of their
taskmasters. Indeed, I know their sufferings."*   —Exodus 3:7

There are very few places today in the world where you can
find people living in a monoculture. Worldwide migration has
made diversity a challenging gift in any rural, urban, peaceful,
or conflict-ridden area. Think of how many people you know
in your own town, neighborhood, or community who come
from a different ethnic background. Wherever there are differences there will be conflict. It is a normal part of life. How we
choose to approach the conflict can lead us deeper into conflict or can lead us into beautiful and enduring relationships
and a deeper understanding of ourselves.

As part of the Maryknoll Sisters Peace Team, my sisters and
I share our experience of intercultural living with the people
we meet and work with in Kenya. We believe building relationships is one way to work through conflict and create a stronger
society. The readings for this Sunday give us encouragement
and hope in this work. In Exodus, Moses approaches a burning bush out of curiosity, to find he is on holy ground, and he
encounters God. He goes beyond his fear to engage the voice
he hears, and receives the message of God.

In the Gospel, Jesus tells a parable with a beautiful message
of hope. The people come to Jesus with news of killing and

disaster, not unlike the events we hear of and experience today. It is not because they are sinners that they suffered, Jesus tells us. But then he still implores the people to change their ways or suffer the same as the others. The parable of the fig tree gives us a hint as to how we might change our ways. The tree is not producing, and the master wants it cut out. But the gardener suggests giving it another chance, to cultivate it, to fertilize it. It may still bear fruit.

In December 2007, following presidential elections, violence broke out in Kenya. The violence took on an ethnic appearance, tribe against tribe. In Kenya, forty-six different ethnic groups coexist. All were affected in some way by the violence, but only four or five were actively involved in committing the violence. Looking at the situation more critically, we can say that the causes were more economic, political, and land-related than ethnic differences. But those in power strategized to use people's ethnic identity to incite the conflict, creating a situation to their benefit. Political, government, and local leaders rally their power base around ethnic identity and blame other ethnic groups for the economic situation, land abuses, or developmental neglect, and give money to jobless youth to commit crimes.

The people most affected are the grassroots communities, the local citizen, those who are poor and marginalized. Those who had learned to live together in diverse communities out of economic necessity found that they could no longer trust their neighbor, no longer buy vegetables from the same shop, and no longer pass through one neighborhood to the next on the way to work without being threatened. Like the fig tree in the parable, the thriving diverse community was no longer fruitful. It was dark, dangerous, and full of hate. Many people lost hope.

As political leaders negotiated national peace, the citizens needed healing and reconciliation to rebuild relationships. The Maryknoll Sisters Peace Team began facilitating conversations, creating space for people to talk with others, of their hopes, dreams, fears, and feelings. We cultivated relationships and nourished them with time, reflection, and listening. We encourage people to listen to others before judging, to put aside their stereotypes, to think before they said something or reacted to another. By working on relationships with others, it is possible to cultivate our relationships, like the fig tree, to become fruitful encounters. If we avoid others who are different from us, it is painful for us and for them; it bears no fruit, and becomes a source of conflict, hatred, and fear.

Like Moses in the book of Exodus, who hid his face lest he see God, the people we gathered had great fear in coming together in a diverse group. They wanted to hide their names (which indicate ethnic background); they wanted to listen before they spoke what was truly in their heart. One participant took the risk and shared that the tribal conflict had even shown up between her fellow church members and how tragic it was that the people they trusted and had relationships with before elections were now enemies. People stayed, as Moses did, to listen and then to share their experiences. They overcame the fear of knowing the other, of building relationships with someone different than "me."

Moses found God in the burning bush; he met God as I AM. Had Moses given into his fear, he would have fled from God. But he was attracted by the mystery of a bush aflame that was not being consumed. Are we curious about those different from us? Each person we meet is a mystery to be discovered. We should approach new relationships as if we are on holy ground.

Fourth Sunday of Lent

Larry Rich, former Maryknoll lay missioner

Peru

Joshua 5:9, 10–12; Psalm 34:2–7; Second Corinthians 5:17–21;
Luke 15:1–3, 11–32

*Now the tax collectors and sinners were coming near to listen to
him. And the Pharisees and the scribes were grumbling and saying, "This fellow welcomes sinners and eats with them."*
—*Luke 15:1–2*

Once again Jesus presents a Gospel that turns our ideas of how
things are supposed to be upside down. We warm to the concept of reconciliation in Paul's letter, which may create for us
a comforting sense of peace and tranquility. But do we really
understand what we must do to be part of that New Creation?
Do we grasp just how upending it is when Paul says the old
things have passed away?

When the Pharisees and scribes say that Jesus welcomes sinners and eats with them, it is not a mild statement: it is an asser-
tion of the established order of things over Jesus' approach.
The Pharisees were accustomed to pronouncing on Mosaic
law and were by and large respected by observant Jews.

The sinners they refer to were the people with whom
upright Jews did not hang out. We find it easy to understand
that this class of nonpersons included prostitutes, thieves, hea-
thens, and the "unchurched" of the times.

But others mentioned here and there in the Gospel as seen
in Jesus' company pose more of a challenge. Tax collectors
were considered traitors doing the Roman Empire's dirty
work for pay. There was at least one officer of the military

occupation. Not to mention that Jesus may have had in his own inner circle a Zealot—a member of a group that sought the violent overthrow of Roman rule, using assassination and what could be called terrorist tactics.

So there is Jesus, unapologetically conversing with genuine social and religious outcasts. His point in doing so is, of course, that every person is of value to God, and that society and religion should be finding ways to count people in rather than out. But he also associates with people who represented threats to the very sacred culture and social order of Israel. He was in dialogue with first-century fascists and their terrorist opponents—it all was quite disturbing to the pious.

The hope is, of course, that the Zealot who is affirmed as a human being will cease to terrorize others. We can assume Simon the Zealot did or he would not have stayed with Jesus. But one doesn't really know that such a thing will happen, and in some ways it sounds naïve to think it will. Therein lies the distance between the old order of things and the new—a gap crossed only via the hard work of reconciliation.

Reconciliation in today's world is anything but a task for the faint of heart. But it is the path to genuine security.

I worked at a church human rights center in Peru throughout the years of a war between the Maoist Shining Path rebels, who employed terror as a tactic with tragic frequency, and a military that sought to crush their enemy with a brutality that often encompassed the innocent. By the end of it all almost seventy thousand people had perished.

I was privileged to know people in Peru who were not afraid to engage whomever they could to save lives and move the country towards peace, even though it be by inches at a time. It felt at times like we were enveloped in darkness—good people, including community leaders of all sorts, were being killed. Yet there were those who could stubbornly envision a different order of things.

They were human rights lawyers, church workers, neighborhood leaders, university professors, trade unionists, peasant farmers, and journalists—people from all sectors of society. They would try to establish lines of communication when doing so could be seen as blocking the revolution by one side and treason by the other. In a country in which relationships are key to getting anything done, they reached across the barriers to other persons.

They had no illusions about success with the most extreme representatives of either side, but there were instances in which they did connect with the humanity of an officer or a rebel leader and lives were spared. Perhaps more important are the other connections that were made across class, party, and other lines. Reconciliation among former adversaries or even people who simply did not know or care about each other became the backbone of resistance to violence and evil. It was a resistance that never used weapons—not because of an abstract ideal, but because weapons did not lead to safety for people.

This all may seem a way off from what comes to mind when we hear the word "reconciliation." However, the writer of the first reading from Joshua seems to say that though sometimes in a period of great social crisis we may need to be nourished and sustained by God directly, the normal route in our lives in common is through the most earthly of things. Hungry people can no longer be fed by manna; they live by the harvest of the land and the bread baked from its grain.

So, too, real security in our divided society and world comes only by way of the arduous path towards reconciliation with whole groups of people we see as not sharing our values. We might even fear them. This does not mean we abandon our beliefs, and it demands the most of our intelligence and courage. On a collective level, it might mean talking with fascists or terrorists or their equivalents, just as Jesus and my Peruvian colleagues did.

Fifth Sunday of Lent

Sr. Theresa Baldini, MM

Southern Sudan

Isaiah 43:16–21; Psalm 126:1–6; Philippians 3:8–14; John 8:1–11

When they kept on questioning him, he straightened up and said to them, "Let anyone among you who is without sin be the first to throw a stone at her." —John 8:7

All the readings today are reflected in Jesus' words to the woman caught in adultery. He did not condemn her, but said, "Go your way."

In many parts of Africa, including Sudan, where I lived for several years, arranged marriages, forced marriages, and child marriages are still prevalent. Children and young women are given away to uncles and cousins, usually men who are much older than they. The young women do not have a choice. Parents and other family or clan members decide to whom they will be given in marriage, sometimes with the aim of keeping the wealth in the extended family. When parents are very poor, they sometimes sell their daughters to the highest bidders.

Unfortunately, girls and women are taught that marriage is the only way through which a female can gain status in her community. Marriage is considered to be a "safe haven" where partners are supposedly faithful to each other. However, there still are so many areas in Africa, particularly in Sudan, where men can have as many wives or mistresses as they wish. Women have to prove their fertility at all costs in many of our communities. Men pressure women to have children, and women bow to the pressure in the hope that the father of their child will marry them.

The woman caught in adultery in today's Gospel was considered marginalized, but where was the man who was with the woman? The men of Jesus' time never thought that other males were accountable for having illicit sex. Jesus' actions speak deeply to the humanity of the woman; he does not get caught up in the arguments of the men who brought her to him. The first reading from Isaiah reflects Jesus' attitude toward the woman: "Do not remember the former things, or consider the things of old. I am about to do a new thing; now it springs forth, do you not perceive it?"

The readings made me think of one of our dear friends in Narus, South Sudan, a forty-four-year-old Sudanese woman named Anna, who is beautiful, hardworking, and a faith-filled Catholic. She cooks for some of the personnel and guests on the diocesan compound. She is a mother of six children from eight years to twenty years old. Her husband died suddenly, and as is the custom in her tribe, her husband's brother sent word that he would take her into his home as his fourth wife.

Anna met with us in great distress as she did not want to involve herself nor her children with her husband's brother. We encouraged her to meet with her brother-in-law and family and explain that as a Catholic she did not wish to have another husband and that she was able to support her family on the small salary she received from cooking.

It was a miracle that the family accepted Anna's request, but they felt that they needed to abide by custom and asked Anna to leave the hut she had lived in with her husband and children when he was alive. All the family's belongings, including the hut, now belonged to his brother. For a time, Anna and three of her children were able to share a section of a hut belonging to a friend. Anna's three oldest children are living with Anna's mother in a refugee camp in Uganda, where they attend school.

Anna's acceptance of these demands made me think of St. Augustine's words, "Those who have God can afford to be poor": she could let go of what seemed to be essential needs. Anna and others here in South Sudan are teaching me to live with enough. They are revealing to me that there are two things that can displace the human spirit—wanting more of everything and not knowing the meaning of "having enough."

When we heard of Anna's predicament, we were able to help her build a small dwelling for herself and her three children with a small gift we received. Anna's new house is made from mud bricks that have been baked in the sun, and it has two rooms with small windows and a dirt floor. Anna was radiant with joy when she brought us to see her home; she feels that this home is truly a castle for her. We thank God for making "something new" for her and her children! Indeed, Anna's courage is giving options to other women in similar situations.

Anna teaches me a theology of life that transcends difficulties and through solidarity in our common struggle makes hope an ongoing gift that is given and received. Living among the people of South Sudan, especially the women, I have learned from their suffering that a salient part of being human is to see that no one suffers alone, that no pain goes unnoticed, and that no pain is without meaning. God's signature is scrawled across the face of every person—for each of us is the Beloved of God!

Palm Sunday

Linda Unger, Editor, *Maryknoll Magazine* and
Revista Maryknoll, 1993–2010

Isaiah 50:4–7; Psalm 22:8–9, 17–20, 23–24; Philippians 2:6–11;
Luke 22:14–23:56

*"This is my body which is given for you. Do this in remembrance
of me."*   —*Luke 22:19*

March 24 marks the anniversary of the death of San Salvador
Archbishop Oscar Arnulfo Romero. It was always striking to
me that Romero should have been killed by an assassin's bullet
the Monday before Palm Sunday and that his funeral, which
was interrupted by more bloodshed, should have occurred the
Monday following—the doorway to Holy Week—in 1980.
Romero's commitment to peace was unmoved by the violence
that continually threatened him in the last three years of his
life. Instead, he echoed Christ's own response to violence,
"Stop! No more of this!"

Oscar Romero was a quiet, soft-spoken man, "except
when he was in the pulpit," recalls Franciscan Brother Octa-
vio Durán, who was a seminarian in El Salvador at the time
Romero was consecrated archbishop. Romero's homilies were
long, bold, detailed teachings, rooted in scripture and in the
life of the "church of God" in El Salvador.

Week after week, he recalled by name the victims of the
growing violence in the country. Though I did not know
Romero, nor those who were killed, tortured, or disappeared
in the late 1970s, I used to listen to tapes of his homilies and
pray with the litany of victims, until the tapes finally wore
out. I understood this holy man to say that if we forget those
who suffer violence at the hands of others, we run the risk

of dismissing their humanity, our own, and that even of the perpetrators.

Having passed through his own mighty conversion, Romero constantly called the church to a change of heart. Shortly before his death, he told a reporter, "You can tell the people that if they succeed in killing me, I forgive and bless those who do it." Romero thus put into words the action of Jesus in the garden of his capture when Jesus raised his hand to heal and restore the ear of the high priest's servant, cut off by an overzealous disciple, whom Jesus corrected in that same motion.

In our day, we remain tempted by violence, whether as self-defense, self-indulgence, or revenge. Today, armed conflict or all-out war rages in over twenty countries around the world. There is violence in our homes, in our neighborhoods, and in our church and other houses of worship. There is violence in our language, music, and art. The meek are considered weak and the brash bold.

Yet how much more courage and boldness does it take to both name the violence and victims in our lives, society, and world and to forgive the perpetrators? Even in small, day-to-day conflicts we find this difficult. It is much easier to ignore or justify the event, sweep it under the emotional rug, or cathartically lash out at the wrongdoer with no real intention of evoking change.

Jesus models for us the way of peace when he identifies himself with the poor and those who suffer and calls persecutors to conversion through forgiveness. In Luke's Gospel, Jesus' lament over his abandonment by God is replaced by words of forgiveness for those who mock, beat, and crucify him: "Father, forgive them, for they do not know what they are doing."

The path he walks is made of love, humility, and the healing grace of forgiveness. In the letter to the Philippians, Paul underscores this when he tells how Jesus "emptied himself, taking the form of a slave, being born in human likeness. And being found in human form, he humbled himself and became obedient to the point of death—even death on a cross."

Romero chose to follow Jesus and to accept the consequences of a life of service to the poor, a life that could be violently unpopular with the powers of the time. Yet, he did not respond to violence with a call for more violence but, rather, trusted in love. "I did not hide my face from insult and spitting. The LORD GOD helps me; therefore I have not been disgraced," as the prophet Isaiah says.

This same choice confronts us today.

Holy Thursday

Angel Mortel, former Maryknoll lay missioner

Brazil

Exodus 12:1–8, 11–14; Psalm 116:12–13, 15–18;
First Corinthians 11:23–26; John 13:1–15

Then he poured water into a basin and began to wash the disciples' feet and to wipe them with the towel that was tied around him.   —John 13:5

"Let me be a servant to you. Let me be as Christ to you. Pray that I might have the grace to let you be my servant too." When my husband and I chose "The Servant Song" by Richard Gillard for our wedding ceremony, we hoped it would set the tone for our lifelong relationship—a relationship in which we commit ourselves to give to each other completely, but also to be open to receiving graciously from the other. As Jesus reminds us in today's Gospel, all relationships call us to give and receive. As Peter's surprise at Jesus' teaching demonstrates, sometimes being open to being served is more difficult than serving. True relationship and connection happen when the service goes both ways. Everyone has something to offer.

When I was a missioner in São Paulo, Brazil, I met a woman named Maria do Socorro. She had seven children and was raising them alone because her husband was in jail. I noticed that Socorro lived pretty isolated from the larger community, and asked others why. They said that her husband was a notoriously dangerous drug trafficker and many in the community feared him, so they stayed away.

Socorro worked as a housekeeper in downtown São Paulo, a two-hour bus ride from where she lived. Her kids ranged in age from two to twelve years old. She couldn't afford child care for the younger kids, so she locked them up in the house alone and left the older ones in charge.

One morning when the older kids were at school, the four younger kids were locked in the house alone. Socorro had instructed the older kids to take the house key with them because she didn't want the younger ones out in the street. The seven-year-old, Roberto, wanted to make coffee for breakfast. He boiled a pot of water, and when he poured the water the pot broke and the scalding hot water fell on the leg of his five-year-old sister, Mariana. She went into shock and Roberto had to get help, but he couldn't get out. So he ran to the backyard, struggled over a wall and fell into his neighbor's yard. She wasn't home so he squeezed through the bars on her front gate and was able to get someone to call for emergency help. Mariana spent two months in the hospital.

The story spread quickly in the community and people were moved. They could relate to Socorro's struggles of raising kids alone, to her frustration with not finding work close to home, and to her fear of the street violence. After the accident, Socorro was very reluctant to leave her kids at home alone, so she quit her job and this made her daily struggle to survive all the more difficult. Her daughter desperately needed follow-up care and Socorro couldn't always get it. Mariana had to wear a special sock on her leg that held the skin in place as it healed. Months passed, and Socorro couldn't save enough money for the sock. In an act of solidarity, our small faith community, Santo Eugenio, raised the money to help Socorro buy the sock. Many people in the community are very poor, but they offered what they could. They collected close to US$300, mostly in coins.

Socorro was overwhelmed by the parish's generosity. Several members of the community started to help her with child care and food. She wanted to give back in some way and asked how. I remember the parish leaders telling her that they were there to serve her and that she didn't need to do anything or give anything in return. I remember a private conversation with one of the leaders in which he said to me, "What could she give us anyway? She can't read and she doesn't have any time with all those kids." He and the rest of the community seemed closed to receiving anything from her.

Despite the parish's resistance to accept any help from Socorro, she found several small ways to serve. She washed the altar cloths every week; she swept the church after Mass; she started going to Mass; she sent her kids to catechism classes; she sent her older kids to help with church events. Slowly, Socorro became an integral part of the faith community. The relationship of mutual giving and receiving continued as the parish helped Socorro get through lean times without a job, and she continued to help with cleaning and participating in the community.

The Portuguese word *socorro* means "help" in English. When the community was able to accept her openly, to accept her *socorro*, the relationship deepened because there was giving and receiving. By washing each other's feet and by letting others wash our feet we build the new creation with mutual love and service to one another.

Good Friday

Sr. Claudette LaVerdiere, MM

Maryknoll, N.Y.

Isaiah 52:13–53:12; Psalm 31:2, 6, 12–13, 15–17, 25;
Hebrews 4:14–16; 5:7–9; John 18:1–19:42

*So they took Jesus; and carrying the cross by himself, he went
out to what is called The Place of the Skull, which in Hebrew
is called Golgotha. There they crucified him, and with him two
others, one on either side, with Jesus between them.*

—John 19:16–18

All the readings on Good Friday focus on the arrest of Jesus,
his innocence, and what happened after he was seized and
bound. From the relative safety and calm of our U.S. environment, we may spiritualize Good Friday, blithely thinking
of it as a one-time event, long ago—until we are jolted from
our complacency by accounts of human communities awash
in corruption, intimidation, and torture and what that means
for millions of our sisters and brothers throughout the world.
Like Jesus, they too are innocent. Oppressed and condemned,
they are taken away, cut off from the land of the living. Who
knows, who cares, and who remembers? In a recent update,
Sister Mary Frances Kobets, MM, brings the particularly raw
suffering of the people of Zimbabwe, especially the orphans
who are her special predilection, into our daily consciousness.

When the Zimbabwe dollar became defunct, the rulers
declared the U.S. dollar and the South African rand the official currency. But who has any of those precious monies to
purchase foodstuffs, now a bit more available but completely
unaffordable? "The majority of the population has just a few

U.S. dollars to rub together, or none," writes Sr. Fran. Water, the *sine qua non* of life, is drastically in short supply; electricity is a luxury of the past; hospitals run out of aspirin and pharmacists shamelessly dispense it at US$3 for 12 tablets; miners who work in hazardous conditions earn US$20 per month while managers rake in $800; a collapsed education system leaves teachers seriously underpaid and students, the worthy recipients "of purposeful education for intellectual and practical development," with languid instruction; veterinary services in this agricultural country are nonexistent in rural areas for lack of vehicles and supplies; funding for management and conservation of wildlife programs has dried up, giving poachers free rein, etc., etc. The desperate lack of services and goods is coupled with intimidation and reprisals. Corruption feeds corruption. Sr. Fran's sober assessment of this chaos? "Zimbabwe is not recognizable."

Even in a country where many simply do not survive, it was decidedly good news when, in December 2009, President Obama presented that year's Robert F. Kennedy Human Rights Award to Magodona Mahlangu and her organization, Women of Zimbabwe Arise (WOZA). At the time of the award, Sr. Fran wrote: "This recognition is a Christmas 'gift' for Zimbabweans. In response to suffering, intimidation, and torture these women and their leader have organized peaceful resistance opposing rape and violence. Mahlangu said that the $30,000 award will help the Bulawayo-based group to deepen the human rights and advocacy work." She added, "While this amount does not go far in Zimbabwe, the award is appreciated and in the right place."

Much of whatever good news there is in Zimbabwe revolves around Sr. Fran's ministry for young children orphaned by AIDS, Orphans' Education and Agricultural Support. Run by a tight-knit team of Zimbabweans, the group reaches out to young children, many of whom are "heads of households," responsible for their younger brothers and sisters. Some may be fortunate to have a grandparent or another relative, an aunt, an uncle, or a benign neighbor, but most have to fend for themselves. As Sr. Fran interviews each child, she communicates her love, infusing them with hope. She elicits from them a maturity far beyond their years as they partner with her and the team in the right use of the food, clothing, medical care, particularly for those born HIV-positive, and the school fees they will receive, as well as the seeds and agricultural techniques that will make them self-reliant. The team's belief in these young children gives them a future, and their compassion visibly transforms them. The team's dependable dedication, consummate expertise, and love for each child complete the picture. When I visited Sr. Fran a few years ago, I saw the children's radiant smiles in their zest for life. They showed me what hope looks like.

In Zimbabwe, just when you think the situation cannot get worse, it does. What makes it possible for Sr. Fran and her team to be so hopeful in such forsaken situations? How do they carry on day after day? For one, they believe in the resurrection! On that first Good Friday the disciples of Jesus lived through the most ominous day of their lives. It was exceedingly dark—until they experienced Jesus alive in their midst. While resurrection does not take away the pain of Good Friday, nor of all the Good Fridays in the world throughout the ages, it proclaims that no human situation is beyond redemption and that every human being is worthy of our total self-gift. No greater love . . .

The situation of the little team in Zimbabwe is best reflected in Psalm 31, which we pray today. As the Psalmist names all the horrors, he invariably comes back to: "In my distress I called upon the Lord; to my God I cried for help. From his temple he heard my voice, and my cry to him reached his ears." So strong is Sr. Fran's belief in this faithful God, that she unabashedly ended her 2009 Christmas letter with this wish: May you find joy in your heart, peace in your soul, love in your life.

Easter Sunday

Sacha Bermudez Goldman, SJ,
former Maryknoll lay missioner

Tanzania and Cambodia

Acts 10:34, 37–43; Psalm 118:1–2, 16–17, 22–23;
Colossians 3:1–4; John 20:1–9

*Then the other disciple, who reached the tomb first, also went in,
and he saw and believed, for as yet they did not understand the
scripture, that he must rise from the dead.*   —John 20:9

Today's Gospel begins with the discovery by Mary Magdalene of Jesus' empty tomb. Although perhaps expected for an
Easter Sunday liturgy, there is no account of an appearance
of the risen Lord (though Jesus' resurrection is mentioned in
the other two readings). Later, of course, Mary will meet the
risen Lord. Now, following her discovery, she comes running
to tell the other disciples. Her running and her mournful cry,
"They have taken my Lord and I do not know where they have
laid him," bespeak the anguish of continuing love and loss.
The inference is that some human agency (the gardener, the
authorities, grave robbers) have perpetrated this final indignity
on the Lord; even in death his body is to have no peace. So
we are left with this tremendous sense of emptiness and loss.

In Luke's account of this story Peter and the "other disciple" likewise set out on a "race" of anxious love. The "other
disciple" arrives first, but does not enter the tomb immediately; rather, he bends down and sees on the ground only the
linen cloths in which Jesus' body was wrapped. When Peter
goes in, he sees something else: the cloth that covered Jesus'
face, rolled up neatly in a place by itself. As the other disciple
now enters and sees the complete picture, he realizes this is a

sign: grave robbers do not bother to fold up neatly clothing they leave behind! And here the Gospel tells us that "he saw and he believed." He did not see the risen Jesus, but he saw enough to remember the scriptural prophecy that the Messiah would rise from the dead, and thus came to faith in the resurrection.

This "other disciple" stands in there for all of us, believers of subsequent generations. Unlike Mary Magdalene, Peter, and even the insistent Thomas, we do not actually see or feel or touch the risen Lord, and yet we believe! We can see emptiness and absence not as failure and loss but, in the light of scripture, as mysterious evidence of God's power to bring life out of death, not only in Jesus on that first Easter morning, but also today in so many people who strive to overcome pain and loss in their own lives.

The experience of many landmine survivors in various parts of the world speaks loudly of this mysterious evidence of the divine power to bring life out of death. Wiboonrat is like any other "normal" person and in a crowd no one would notice anything strange about her. Only a careful look would reveal that she wears a prosthetic leg.

> I stepped on a landmine one day when I was out with my father, brother, and sister, cutting bamboo not far from our village [in Thailand]. I'd cut sixty-nine bamboo stalks. I only needed one more and then I could go back home. As I reached for that last bamboo stalk, I stepped on a landmine. Hearing the blast, my brother and sister ran to help me, but I shouted to them to stay back, as there could be more landmines around. I dragged myself about fifty meters to a safe area. I was taken to hospital for an operation, and when I woke up afterwards I found that I had lost my left leg below the knee. At

the time I had two children. Soon after the accident
my husband divorced me because of the loss of my
leg. Since then, I started to take care of my children alone, even though my mobility was greatly
reduced and life became very difficult because I was
so slow. A job that other people could finish in one
day might take me eight to ten days to finish.

Wiboonrat's spirit of courage, strength, resilience, and
hope have been a great example to those around her. About
ten years ago, government and village leaders invited her to
join education and training meetings on persons with disabili-
ties at district and provincial levels. There she met others in
similar circumstances as hers, though she also found that there
were many in worse situations—some of them could not move
or speak; some did not have shelter or food to eat. She then
became the chairperson of the persons-with-disability organization in her district. Today she continues to work tirelessly
for their cause. She has represented Thailand's landmine survivors in meetings at provincial, national, and international
levels. "I might be disabled," she says, "but my heart isn't."

And so today we celebrate this Easter Sunday with great joy.
We celebrate the resurrection of our Lord and we celebrate
the new life that has been offered to us through the gift of
God's love in the death and resurrection of Jesus. Jesus is the
hope we have in us. The hope that despite the difficulties,
pain, suffering, and darkness that we encounter in our world,
the light of Christ's resurrection can triumph and will triumph
over this darkness. And so, as the other disciple, we are called
to see and believe—see not with physically "disabled" eyes,
but with eyes of faith and love, giving us a glimpse of the Spirit
of God in each one of us. Our eyes might be lacking, might be
"disabled," but our hearts are not.

Second Sunday of Easter

Sr. Maria Rieckelman, MM

Washington, D.C.

Acts 5:12–16; Psalm 118:2–4, 13–15, 22–24;
Revelation 1:9–11a, 12–13, 17–19; John 20:19–31

"Have you believed because you have seen me? Blessed are those who have not seen and yet have come to believe."   —*John 20:29*

Jesus came to heal all those sick in body, mind, and spirit and to call his followers to be healers. His mercy and compassion opened hearts and minds in ways that dispelled fear. Further, his appearance to the Apostles after he was raised from the dead filled them with courage that helped them overcome their fear, discouragement, and loss. It helped them gradually to trust—to believe that he could and would be with them in a new, though transformed way.

Today's readings are steeped in the healing message of Jesus, his mercy, his patient, compassionate love of us despite our resistance, our unbelief.

Thomas was not with the other disciples when Jesus first appeared in their locked upper room after he was raised from the dead. Thomas did not believe the others; he needed proof by seeing and feeling the wounds inflicted on Jesus. Jesus appeared once again through locked doors to visit with his close friends—disciples all, who were still full of fear because of their close association with Jesus and uncertainty about their future. Thomas was with them this time, and Jesus approached him gently, lovingly letting him feel the wounds of his hands and touch his pierced side. This proof of course convinced Thomas and relieved his doubt. Jesus did not scold him for his doubting but helped him to see and understand his new reality.

How often God is patient with us through our lack of faith and need for clarity. For us so often "seeing is believing," which means that we live in doubt, uncertainty, and deep-seated fear much of our lives. The belief that the Resurrection evokes in us is that Jesus lives in the fullness of God's Spirit. Thomas and the other disciples were beginning to realize that the healing mystery of Jesus challenged them to be healers themselves; they were to heal their neighbors; to serve the least among them; to offer compassion to the most needy and ignored; to know that they are Jesus still hanging on the cross. So often in our lives we are called to believe in things unseen, in promises not yet fulfilled, in healing that seems beyond belief, in possibilities not yet realized, or understood.

In January 2010 and in March 2011, the whole world community was actually absorbed in the heartbreaking damage of Haiti's earthquake and Japan's earthquake, tsunami, and nuclear accident. How could we possibly respond to such indescribable turmoil, devastation, loss, and pain! For the living, for those buried alive, for relatives too far away to relieve the pain of their loved ones, how and what were they to believe! So much agony, so much life-changing injury, such unquenchable pain! Yet we were challenged to embrace an all-loving God suffering in the people of Haiti and Japan; calling us to be healers who could help those whose lives have been torn asunder to believe that they can heal and be healed. The world struggled to help them believe that in their losses they will eventually find their way to recover, to regroup, to heal and live again.

We ask ourselves where our faith would be in such circumstances and continue to pray deeply for those who were caught

in this enormous disruption of human life. One woman res-
cued after a week of burial under her building was murmuring
prayers and singing a song. This pure and simple resilience of
faith buried deep inside her amazes and challenges us. We pray
to be like this woman, living each day with its large or small
struggles; God's Spirit will help us find our way to heal and
be healed.

May we become more and more an Easter people, believing
in the small and large resurrections in our lives day by day. If
seeing is believing, and not seeing yet believing is indeed the
stuff of faith, may the inspiration of the resurrected Jesus lead
us to an ever more profound belief in the healing power of
love and compassion towards all people and in all people!

Third Sunday of Easter

Bro. John Beeching, MM

Thailand

Acts 5:27–32, 40–41; Psalm 30:2, 4–6, 11–13;
Revelation 5:11–14; John 21:1–19 or 21:1–14

When they had finished breakfast, Jesus said to Simon Peter,
"Simon son of John, do you love me more than these?"
                                                        —John 21:15

Today's Gospel recounts the third appearance of Jesus to his disciples after the resurrection, this time on the seashore in Galilee. After they've eaten breakfast, Jesus takes Peter aside to talk to him. Although Peter had been present at the other post-resurrection appearances of Jesus, this is the first opportunity they are alone together since Peter's denial of Jesus. John—never far from the master's side—overhears the conversation and recounts it, the account of the commissioning of Peter.

We know the conversation well. Jesus three times asks Peter whether he truly loves him; each time he is given assurance of Peter's love, he commands him to shepherd his sheep, to tend his flock. And Jesus goes on to indicate the cost involved in being faithful to this command: it is to cost Peter his life.

While the Gospel this morning recounts the particular commissioning of Peter, each one of us is likewise asked the same question by Jesus: "Do you love me?" And each of us with our response is commissioned to tend to one another's needs. In fact, Jesus makes this commission the very sign of those who follow him: "By the love you bear for one another shall all know you are my disciples."

We live in a very different world today than that in which John's Gospel was written. In our community and workplaces we rub shoulders with Buddhists, Muslims, Taoists, Hindus, a great plurality of peoples, all of whom merit our love, respect, and service. How well Pope John Paul II put it when speaking to peoples of various faiths gathered in Assisi for prayer: "The differences [between faiths] are a less important element, when confronted with the unity which is radical, fundamental and decisive. . . . God would like the developing history of humanity to be a fraternal journey in which we accompany one another towards the transcendent goal that God sets for us."

Much of my work during the past twenty years in Thailand has been with Mon refugees, an ethnic minority in flight from civil war in the south of Burma, which is called Myanmar today. Among these refugees were Buddhist monks who asked me to work alongside them in a small monastery in Bangkok that served as a shelter for many of the refugees fleeing at that time. The young monks had carried with them a number of victims wounded in the first wave of fighting, and hearing I had a nursing background, they sought my help. This first wave of refugees was soon joined by an unending stream of others, rice farmers, students, and monks, all fleeing from burned out villages, pillage, rape, and forced labor.

As you might imagine, I felt utterly overwhelmed by what I was being asked to respond to: cases of torture, landmine victims, war wounded, malaria cases, among others. Some we managed to help, others died either in the hospital or simply on the floor of the monastery as we held them, while softly chanting the Buddhist scripture in Pali.

God never gives us more than we can handle. Almost immediately, a Maryknoll lay missioner, Vicki Amour Hileman, offered to work in the temple, attending to some of the most seriously injured. There were volunteers, too, who helped with filing petitions with UNHCR for refugee recognition and who taught English to those selected for resettlement.

I really felt I was doing enough ministering to the medical needs of these refugees, but the monks kept pressing me to join them in protest outside the Burmese embassy. One time after attempting unsuccessfully to treat a young man who had been badly tortured, I remarked to the monks, "I've done all I can."

"No, you haven't," remarked one of the novice monks. "You've failed to protest for what was done to him."

"I can't!" I replied. "As a foreigner, I have a Thai visa, which I could lose for demonstrating in front of an embassy. You are undocumented and have nothing to lose."

"You are quite right," replied the monk softly, "we are undocumented and have nothing to lose, but we do have family members back in Burma, and if we were to be identified by Burmese military intelligence, our kin would pay the price."

A wave of shame swept over me, and I found myself standing beside the monks in their protest outside the embassy; my fear was gone.

At times, living the Gospel demands more than mere kindness to others. We need to understand that our voices need to be heard by lawmakers who daily make decisions that impact whether those living in poverty live with justice, dignity, and rights.

In today's reading from Acts, we find Peter and his companions being flogged in the council chambers of the priests for continuing to speak out for what they believe; they refuse to be silenced. Sometimes speaking out exacts a price, but then, so does silence in the presence of injustice.

So this was the flock I tended in Thailand, made up of village refugees and a beleaguered band of barefoot Buddhist monks. Though not of common faith, we shared common bonds of caring for those in need—I out of belief in the Gospel, the monks out of the practice of meditation and the observance of monastic precepts. They were models of quiet compassion, calm concern and care. In the pathways of salvation we needed each other. In time I came to understand what Bishop Mansap of Thailand meant when he told his fellow bishops from the floor of the Asian Synod of Bishops in Rome: "Working with my Buddhist friends in the field of human development, justice, and peace, I feel inspired by their simplicity of life, their openness, their humane relationships, their unassuming ways in dealing with each other. This is the Good News that the Buddhists give us. They are evangelizing us."

I wonder how many of us have thought of salvation in those terms, that in the very process of reaching out to peoples of other faiths, or working alongside them for the common good we are being evangelized by them, evangelized by Buddhists, Muslims, Hindus, and Jews, all of us co-pilgrims in our journey home to the Divine. I know that this has been my experience, and that of Vicki, the missioner who worked alongside me with that small band of Buddhist refugee monks. In the book she later wrote relating that experience, Vicki shared, "Whatever salvation means, though in its final form it is a long way off for this world, whenever two strangers look at each other with understanding and love and commit themselves to a journey together, in some way maybe we are already saved."

Fourth Sunday of Easter

Fr. Dennis Moorman, MM

Brazil

Acts 13:14, 43–52; Psalm 100:1–3, 5;
Revelation 7:9, 14–17; John 10:27–30

"My sheep hear my voice. I know them, and they follow me."
—John 10:27

On this fourth Sunday of Easter, when we also observe the World Day of Prayer for Vocations, Jesus is presented to us in the Gospel as the Good Shepherd who cares for his flock. We hear that three things are necessary for one to belong to Jesus' flock. These three qualities might also be considered important characteristics of discipleship, which is at the heart of our Christian vocation. The sheep must listen for the shepherd's voice, establish an intimate relationship of trust with the shepherd, and actively follow where the shepherd leads. In the same way, the disciple must listen to Jesus' voice, nurture a loving relationship with him, and follow in his footsteps. As the people of God, we are the flock that makes up the church and manifests the Gospel of Jesus Christ in the here and now. In my work with Catholic Christian communities I have found that many people understand this aspect of their Christian vocation. However, the first reading highlights another essential aspect of our vocation as Christians that is often overlooked.

In the Acts of the Apostles we read about Paul and Barnabas's first missionary journey to Asia Minor. The early Christians didn't concern themselves only with their own local communities, but understood their vocation to be essentially one of sharing the Good News with others in faraway lands. The Second Vatican Council in 1965 affirmed this when it promulgated *Ad Gentes,* the Decree on the Missionary Activity of the Church, and said: "The Church on earth is by her very nature missionary, since, according to the plan of the Father, she has her origin in the mission of the Son and the Holy Spirit" (*Ad Gentes* no. 2). In Acts we read that at first, Paul and Barnabas's message of Jesus as the way to salvation was well-received by the people. But later when it became clear that this salvation is also extended to the Gentiles, those who were considered "unclean," their message was rejected. Paul and Barnabas were eventually expelled from the territory because of the good news of inclusivity they preached.

Today, as church, we are very devoted to Jesus and seek to live better lives by listening to his Word through scripture and nurturing our relationship with him in the Eucharist. But sometimes the translation into action by walking in Jesus' footsteps is a bigger leap of faith than we are able to make. Do we welcome the "Gentile" or "stranger" among us as Jesus so often did? How do we treat the immigrants crossing our borders looking for a way to make a living and improve life for their own families? Are we able to welcome our gay, lesbian, bisexual, and transgendered brothers and sisters to enrich our faith communities with the special gifts they have to offer? Even though we might have adequate health care for ourselves, do we act with compassion for those who are unable to afford the same level of health care? Are we holding our elected officials accountable to be of service to all of the people, including the poor and excluded of society? We all have our own prejudices and righteous justifications for these. But Jesus crossed the boundaries of discrimination and prejudice of his day and reached out to touch the "untouchables" and welcome them into the fold. Jesus is indeed our Good Shepherd. And Jesus' vocation must become our mission if we are to live as authentic Christians.

When I first arrived at my mission in Brazil, I was impressed by the National Conference of Brazilian Bishops' commitment to including the voice of minority citizens who would otherwise have gone unheard in the political process. During the national presidential elections, the Brazilian bishops organized a national televised debate of the presidential candidates. The president of the Bishops' Conference mediated the questions asked by representatives of various groups such as Afro-Brazilians, indigenous, workers, women, unemployed, etc. I was so impressed by seeing the leadership in the church live out its missionary vocation in such a truly prophetic manner.

At our baptism we are anointed with Holy Oil to carry out a mission. This mission is the essence of our calling or "vocation" as Christians, whether we are young or old, single or married, gay or straight, clergy, religious, or laity—as a Christian community our vocation must be to live the Good News of Jesus Christ and reach out to the excluded and oppressed of our society and give them hope of salvation for a better life, rooted in the Gospel of Jesus Christ.

Fifth Sunday of Easter

Amy Braun, former Maryknoll lay missioner

Bangkok, Thailand

Acts 14:21–27; Psalm 145:8–13; Revelation 21:1–5;
John 13:31–35

*"By this everyone will know that you are my disciples, if you have
love for one another."* —John 13:35

We continue to joyfully celebrate God's new life for us this
Easter season. In the scripture readings for this fifth Sunday
of Easter, we begin to glimpse the Reign of God—a place
of great beauty, harmony, and peace. Most importantly, it is
where God dwells with us. The promise of Emmanuel is fulfilled in Revelation: "See, the home of God is among mor-
tals. He will dwell with them; they will be his peoples, and
God himself will be with them." This sublime vision is one of
renewal, promise, and fulfillment.

In today's Gospel, Jesus gives us an important instruction:
"Love one another. Just as I have loved you, you also should
love one another." This is the final commandment, so simple,
and yet so profound and difficult to practice in our daily lives.
This commandment tells us that our relationship to God is
intimately tied with our relationships to each other. Striving
to express this love is the great privilege of our lives and also
requires sacrifice and responsibility from each one of us. Most
of us live today in a culture that values instant gratification,
wish fulfillment, and individualism; we are influenced by our
culture whether we like it or not. Yet we still have agency and
responsibility within our unique families, communities, cultures, and contexts. Jesus is calling us to love and has given us
a very clear example through his life and ministry.

Our challenge is to follow the example of Jesus to deal with the unique challenges we face in contemporary times. One such challenge, which like so many others did not exist in Jesus' time, is the environmental crisis and global warming. In Asia, people are feeling the effects of climate change in disastrous ways. Snow and glaciers are melting in the Himalayas, which will cause catastrophic floods followed by crippling drought. Flooding and natural disasters are creating hundreds of thousands of "climate refugees" who can no longer survive in their native places. In my ministry in Bangkok, we recently organized a gathering of people from many different religious traditions to discuss how communities of faith should respond to global warming. We found that, despite our different belief and cultures, four main principles guided us.

The first is belief in the integrity of creation. Life and all things good in life have been given to us and we all must exercise not just appreciation, but also stewardship over what we have been blessed to receive.

Second, we believe we are interconnected, creating the need to listen to one another and to find commonalities and shared concerns in differences, and the need to understand the linkages between poverty, justice, and climate change.

Third, we believe in justice for all, through equitable and just access to resources that are becoming scarce due to climate change, and ensuring the poor do not bear a disproportionate burden of climate effects.

Lastly, we will use principled pragmatism in our responses to climate change. We need to ask not only, "Will it work?" but also "Is it right? Is it just?" (*Interfaith Perspectives on Climate Change: Faith Communities in Action* [Bangkok: AMAN, 2009]). I found myself humbled and inspired by this vision developed jointly by Christians, Hindus, Buddhists, Muslims, and people practicing traditional religions.

As disciples of Jesus, we must also frame the question in terms of Jesus' new commandment to us: Love one another as I have loved you. I find myself often asking, "How should we love one another?" but rarely asking, "Who are the others?" Of course my family, my community, my neighbors, and my mission community in Thailand are obviously connected to me. But now our connections extend beyond the people we know. Because this planet is a beautifully interconnected system, our actions also impact our neighbors whom we will never see and know nothing about, encompassing those from all corners of the world and even future generations. Yet it is our responsibility to care for them just the same.

We see how God cares for us, for creation, and especially for the poor and marginalized in our midst. As the body of Christ, we have a sacred duty to care for each other and for the environment. In my own life, how will I humbly fulfill this responsibility to neighbors both nearby and far away? How will I show my discipleship?

As each of us strives to live the new commandment of Jesus, we do so in the knowledge that we are bringing our community one step nearer to the beautiful vision of God's reign, and God is dwelling with us.

Sixth Sunday of Easter

Ted and Maruja Gutmann-Gonzalez,
former Maryknoll lay missioners

Chile

Acts 15:1–2, 22–29; Psalm 67:2–3, 5, 6, 8;
Revelation 21:10–14, 22–23; John 14:23–29

"Those who love me will keep my word, and my Father will love them, and we will come to them and make our home with them." —*John 14:23*

A devastating earthquake and tsunami in Chile in 2010 was experienced by many as an "apocalyptic" moment. And it was, but not in the sense that the world is going to end. Rather, it was a call to each of us, to society in general, and, in fact, to all of humanity to transform ourselves.

The following reflection was written by a friend of ours a week after the earthquake. Vanessa is a social worker who has worked for Catholic Relief Services. In the midst of chaos she opened herself to the Spirit, and like a prophet, teaches and reminds us what is essential in life.

Vanessa's words are a reminder of John's vision of an angel in the reading from the Apocalypses: "And in the spirit he carried me away to a great, high mountain and showed me the city Jerusalem coming down out of heaven from God. It has the glory of God and a radiance like a very rare jewel, like jasper, clear as crystal."

Vanessa wrote, "When I read what people [wrote] on social networks about . . . the earthquake we have experienced, I am surprised, struck, and also hurt. However, for some strange reason, I am also filled with hope. . . .

"This earthquake has left us with cracks that nobody wants to see about our deep social inequalities and the paradigms on which we have built the way we relate to one another.

"Yesterday, a woman started to cry when she received a box of supplies that arrived as a donation to her completely devastated coastal town. When somebody asked why her tears, she said something that really struck me: 'It is very difficult to receive a donation. I always saw these things on TV, but I never thought that one day it would be my turn.' How difficult it is to accept that we are fragile, that we can be on one side or the other of the coin at any given moment, and that our possibility to emerge intact depends upon having solidarity networks. It is hard to accept the fact that 'we are all equal,' we all have the same dignity and equal rights, that we are all people, and that *that* is our only essential and authentic value.

"To be able to recognize that we depend on other beings and that our survival rests upon our interdependent relationship with others and the environment we inhabit is good news in the midst of a social culture that has ingrained in the collective unconscious the idea that each one must take care of himself or herself.

"In a society that has systematically isolated people, exacerbated our individualism, and turned consumerism into our only reference for being and belonging, it is touching and energizing to see images of people who place all that they have onto a common table in order to be shared, who greet each other in the warehouses set up for receiving aid despite not knowing one another, and who work and sweat together in the common task of becoming 'bridges' so that help reaches those who are suffering.

"I feel that something deeply human has moved in us, a collective consciousness that we all belong, that we are all one. In other circumstances, in a different time, this aware-ness was asleep and seldom 'saw.' The awareness that we all participate in the lives of everyone else is something we can recover during moments like this. The knowledge that our success, our achievements, and our privileges are, in part, due to others, opens us to the good news that we are a part of—we belong to—a transcendent reality that encompasses all. And this moves us to the encounter, to the fraternal embrace, to inquire about the names, and become concerned about the reality we are confronting together. It motivates us to feel alive and important, recognized by others, accepted, valued, and discovered in our own human dignity.

"As far as I can see, this earthquake is offering us a unique opportunity: to transform. Transform ourselves personally, opening up to the other. Transform ourselves socially, in com-munity, tending to the needs and reality of those we see near us. Transform the paradigms of our society, to recuperate that which is deeply human in each person.

"If only we can see this opportunity and act consequently, it is highly probable we will advance with strength towards new forms of social behavior, of personal relationships, of bonds with the environment we inhabit. Then a new country would be possible, a new country, where everyone has a place and participation. We may be able to make all things new, to give a true sense to that, which for those of us who believe, means Resurrection.

"I fervently desire that this experience does not leave us the same. We have an opportunity; let's not waste it."

Feast of the Ascension

Fr. Ken Thesing, MM

Kenya

Acts 1:1–11; Psalm 47:2–3, 6–9; Ephesians 1:17–23;
Luke 24:46–53

After his suffering he presented himself alive to them by many
convincing proofs, appearing to them during forty days and
speaking about the kingdom of God. —*Acts 1:3*

Years ago I was called back from my African assignment to
work at our mission center in the United States. A couple of
months later on a particular morning I saw a large sign on the
lawn in front of the building, announcing an employee's forti-
eth birthday. We had a great celebration that day, honoring all
she had done and meant so far in this "first half" or so of life.

I realized how important the number 40 is in our ordinary
daily life. For us Christians the number 40 has real significance. In the Bible it has great symbolic meaning. God sent
40 days of rain in the great flood of Noah's time to purge the
earth of sin; the Jewish people spent 40 years in the desert to
learn to recognize and trust in the God of Abraham, Isaac,
and Jacob, who was leading them from slavery in Egypt to
the promised land; Jesus himself passed 40 days in the desert
preparing to fully recognize, accept, and strengthen himself
to live out a vocation that would lead him ultimately to death
on the cross; and Jesus was present among his Apostles and
disciples for 40 days following his Resurrection, teaching them
to trust in the promise of his abiding presence even though
he would no longer be physically present with them after he
ascended into heaven.

116 FEAST OF THE ASCENSION

In Africa many times I observed how with dances, with drums and songs, and with stories told by the elders among the whole people, the wisdom and truths, the culture and values of the people were passed down from one generation to the next. It was a reality that was not observed physically but it was a truly abiding presence that continued strong in each generation. For our catechumens too who were preparing for baptism, songs and dances and storytelling were important parts of their catechesis, the way of their imbibing and absorbing the reality of the living faith of the Christian community. All of this is also using the familiar and well-understood ways to introduce something new and important.

Today we celebrate the Feast of the Ascension of Jesus. Jesus takes leave of the Apostles and disciples among whom he has lived and preached and taught. He is going to God, to the one he calls Father, and tells the disciples they will receive the Spirit as his abiding presence. And then they are to go out to the whole world, to be witnesses to him and preach and teach and baptize in his name, knowing he is with them.

Just like those early Apostles and disciples, you and I and all Christians receive anew today this commission to "go out" and bear witness to the good news of Jesus. Our challenge is to discern how God is calling each of us, how to concretely carry out this mission of witness we are given.

In this respect in these last days of the Easter season I am reminded of the powerful movie *Schindler's List*, which was based on the life of Oskar Schindler, a nominally Christian man in Germany during the Holocaust. When he learned that thousands of Jews were being sent to concentration camps, he saw a chance for personal gain. He started buying some of them, thinking only to use them as cheap labor in his factories. But soon he found one to be brilliant in finances, another to be a master labor organizer, another proficient in factory management. Another was a beautiful woman to whom he became attracted. He discovered by his experience that the people being sent to camps were not slaves, not subhumans as he and others had been told, that they were like insects or vermin to be squashed and incinerated. In and through his own personal conversion he saw their true humanity. He began to use his own money to buy Jews, not to use them to make him money but to help them to freedom and to save their lives. He used all his money, then all his properties and finally sold all his business interests. Near the end of the movie he breaks down, realizing how little he can do. Some thirteen hundred people made it onto his list, those he had bought and saved from death. The last scene of the movie was recorded at the cemetery. It showed not professional actors and extras, but the real-life children and grandchildren of those people Schindler had saved. In the Jewish tradition, they were putting a rock on his tomb to show that he was not forgotten. As the Talmud says, "Whoever saves a life, it is considered as if he saved an entire world."

In 2010 I completed several years in Southern Sudan having helped to establish and re-establish education programs, village and community schools among refugees recently returned to their homes from wars, and internally displaced persons. I too often thought what we do is to help so few where the need is so great. But at the same time I realized how many people there were among us who now were teachers and educational administrators who were the very ones only a few years earlier who had been in the first schools established in the refugee camps. And I realized again the important thing is not just to focus on those we cannot reach; the important thing is to do what we can. Schindler said at the end of his

life: "If only I had done more; if only I had started earlier."
The lesson for us is: well, start now. And Jesus promises the
disciples and us: "And see, I am sending upon you what my
Father promised; so stay here . . . until you have been clothed
with power from on high" (Luke 24:49).

Pentecost

Barbara Fraser, former Maryknoll lay missioner

Peru

Acts 2:1–11; Psalm 104:1, 24, 29–30, 31, 34;
First Corinthians 12:3–7, 12–13; John 20:19–23

*And suddenly from heaven there came a sound like the rush of
a violent wind, and it filled the entire house where they were
sitting.* —*Acts 2:2*

In the Andean mountains of Peru, a Quechua woman named
Hilaria Supa from Cusco was elected to Congress in 2006.
One day, a tabloid newspaper published a photo of some notes
she had been taking during a session of Congress. The notes
contained spelling errors that were not unusual for someone
whose first language was not Spanish.

The photo touched off a spirited debate. The newspaper
said the errors showed Ms. Supa was not fit to serve in Congress. Other people, however, said the attack on her was a
sign of discrimination in a country that has a large indigenous
population.

Language can be a source of conflict for us today, just as it
was for the people in today's first reading from the Acts of the
Apostles.

Have you ever stood in a busy train or bus station, hearing
people around you speaking foreign languages? Or tried to ask
directions in a country where you did not speak the language?
Carrying on conversations is such a natural and important part
of everyday life that when we cannot do it, we may feel lost
and frightened. We hear words, but we can't understand what

they mean. What are people saying? Are they talking about us? Warning us of danger? Wanting to be our friends?

Language is part of our identity. It enables us to express ourselves and to talk about things that are close to our hearts. There are more than six thousand languages in the world, and they reflect the great diversity of people and cultures on our planet. Sometimes, though, we find that diversity overwhelming. We want to take refuge in the familiar, and we may wish other people were more like us.

Many countries have a dominant language. People who speak a different language may insist that their children speak only the country's main language so they do not suffer discrimination as Congresswoman Supa did. Sometimes, so few people remain who speak a language that it becomes extinct. When that happens, the world loses a cultural treasure.

Ruben Medina, a Huitoto Indian, grew up in a tiny village in the Amazon rain forest in Peru, a three-day journey by river from Iquitos, the nearest city. Unlike Congresswoman Supa's family, his parents did not want him to speak his native language because they thought he would be at a disadvantage later in life. "Our people are losing their customs," he says. By the time he graduated from high school, he spoke no Huitoto.

When he went to college in Iquitos, he met other indigenous students who were proud of their roots. Now when he returns to his community, he asks his grandmother to teach him to speak Huitoto. He learned the worth of his cultural identity from other people who valued their own.

Congresswoman Supa's native Quechua language has many different words for rain, because her people are farmers who depend on the weather for their livelihood in a harsh climate. People who live in the Arctic have many different words for snow, which is the main feature of their environment. These differences are a window through which we gain a different perspective on our world.

Today's feast of Pentecost invites us to give thanks for the differences among us. The different gifts, different opinions, different languages, different foods, different customs, different talents and beliefs and ways of looking at the world.

When the disciples began to speak in different languages, they were able to preach the Good News beyond their own community. But communication is a two-way street. With the ability to speak comes the responsibility to listen. Once we can communicate, once we can understand, we must stop and listen to what others have to say. We have much to learn from people who are different from us. It may take a great deal of effort to set aside our prejudices, to realize, like Ruben Medina did, all people have this right to claim their own identity, which is shaped by their cultural heritage.

When we embrace the diversity in our community, despite our fears, Jesus comes to us, as he did to the disciples in today's Gospel. He stands in our midst, holds out his hands to us, and says, "Peace be with you." He reminds us that we are one body, as St. Paul says, and draws us together around his table.

Today is a good day to reflect on the diversity in our own church community, neighborhood, city, and country. Does the diversity divide us, or do we embrace it? Does it frighten us? Can we draw strength from Jesus' promise of peace, so we can reach out to people who are different from us, stand up for them when they suffer discrimination, share our lives with them, and ask them to share their culture with us?

This Pentecost, let us pray that our church communities become places where all people feel welcome and that they serve as a beacon of hope and a model of peace for our neighborhoods and towns, for our country and our world.

Holy Trinity Sunday

Kathy Morefield, Maryknoll Affiliate

Cambodia

Proverbs 8:22–31; Psalm 8:4–9; Romans 5:1–5; John 16:12–15

Hope does not disappoint us, because God's love has been poured into our hearts through the Holy Spirit that has been given to us.   —Romans 5:5

A Maryknoll lay missioner shared the following story as we headed out to dinner one evening in Phnom Penh. He had just returned from visiting two young Cambodian friends, Chea and Sophy, and their five-month-old son. Chea and Sophy met a couple of years earlier at the non-profit organization for homeless children where they and our friend worked. Chea and Sophy fell in love and decided to marry. Although arranged marriages are the tradition in Cambodia, a growing number of families allow their sons and daughters to marry for love, but not the families of Chea and Sophy. "Absolutely not!" their parents said. Why not? Because Chea was Buddhist and Sophy was Muslim. Despite the fact that the Cham Muslim minority has resided in Cambodia for generations, there is little interaction or cooperation between Buddhists and Muslims.

But the young couple persisted in their decision to marry, and the families reluctantly agreed to meet. Both sets of parents were anxious about the meeting, but when Chea's mother walked into Sophy's home and saw Sophy's mother, she ran to her, hugged her, and began weeping. She told the surprised onlookers that she and Sophy's mother had been in the same work camp in the Khmer Rouge war. During the war millions of Cambodians died from starvation, disease, overwork, torture, and murder. Chea's mother became seriously ill, and Sophy's mother cared for her and nursed her back to health. After the war they were separated, and Chea's mother tried for years to find Sophy's mother to let her know that she had survived and that she was still alive because of her.

Paul said in the letter to the Romans that "God's love has been poured into our hearts through the Holy Spirit that has been given to us."

As I listened to our friend's story, I had no doubt that the Holy Spirit had been working in Southeast Asia; first bringing the two teenage girls together in a time of brutal war and then reuniting them thirty years later through the love of their children.

Today we live in a world racked with tension and division. War, oppression, terror, and retaliation are too often carried out in the name of God or religion. In his book *Radical Grace*, Fr. Richard Rohr writes that God forbids us to accept "as-it-is" in favor of "what-God's-love-can-make-it." To believe in the Resurrection means to cross and transcend boundaries. The Kingdom, or Realm, of God is possible here and now, but we need to first face our fear of the stranger, of the one who is different from or who disagrees with us. We must cross and transcend boundaries as Chea and Sophy did, and as their mothers did before them.

Anything is possible through the grace of the Spirit. In the Gospel reading we heard that the Spirit of Truth will guide you to the truth. Imagine the courage it took for the young Muslim/Buddhist couple to approach their parents. Courage is one of the gifts of the Spirit. Their courage to cross and transcend boundaries will have consequences that affect their families, their communities, and their country. When I asked our Maryknoll friend for permission to share his story he said, "Of course you may use the story. It belongs to the universe and must be told again and again."

Our understanding of the Trinity teaches us about unity in diversity. The love of Chea and Sophy teaches us that crossing and transcending boundaries is possible—in our families, in our communities, in our churches, in our nations, and in the world. In this crossing and transcending we are supported and strengthened by the Spirit who, as we heard in the first reading, plays on the surface of the earth and finds delight in the whole human race.

Some questions we can ask ourselves would be: What can I learn from the example of Chea and Sophy? Where are the boundaries I need to cross and transcend in my own life? What gifts of the spirit do I need to take the first step?

Feast of Corpus Christi

Fr. Raymond Finch, MM

Bolivia

Genesis 14:18–20; Psalm 110:1–4; First Corinthians 11:23–26; Luke 9:11b–17

And taking the five loaves and the two fish, he looked up to heaven, and blessed and broke them, and gave them to the disciples to set before the crowd. And all ate and were filled.

—*Luke 9:16–17*

The first fiesta Mass that I celebrated in the mountains of Peru was in a small Aymara village of no more than a hundred families. It was a four-hour ride by jeep over a very rough dirt road even higher into the mountains than our parish center, which was located at 12,500 feet above sea level. I remember arriving at the village and being greeted with a sumptuous meal. Though my room was an adobe hut with a dirt floor and thatched roof, there were plentiful blankets and a big comfortable bed for the very cold night. The next morning we were all up early to begin the celebrations. The small village was transforming itself into a celebration for at least a thousand people; the fiesta was beginning. The people were poor; they gave everyone the best that they had. The villagers understood the Feast of Corpus Christi as a time to give the best to their friends, neighbors, and visitors. Though ten times the population of the village had arrived for the fiesta, there was plenty for everyone, just like we heard in the Gospel of Luke a few minutes ago.

Throughout the thirty years that I worked among the Aymara and Quechua of Peru and Bolivia, I have never ceased to be amazed at the generosity that they show to visitors and strangers. I have never entered a home in a city or rural community without being offered the very best that they could provide. That generosity has a lot to do with what we are celebrating this Sunday.

The feast of Corpus Christi is the celebration of the presence of Christ in our midst; it is the celebration of the installation of the Eucharist. We remember the words of Jesus at the Last Supper, which we heard in the second reading and which we will hear again later in the consecration during this celebration: "This is my body which will be given up for you; this is the cup of my blood, the blood of the new covenant which will be shed for you and for many. Do this in memory of me." Corpus Christi is the celebration of Christ in the Eucharist. We remember how Jesus gave totally of himself so that we might have life. We recognize Christ present in the transformed bread and wine and we remember his sacrifice. Not as something in the past, two thousand years ago, but as a living sacrifice today that we join ourselves to as Christians, as the Body of Christ. Just as the bread and wine are transformed into the body and blood of Christ so do we pray to be transformed into Christ, to give totally of ourselves so that others might have life. Bread and wine are transformed into the body and blood of Jesus in memory of him, and we offer to give totally of ourselves in memory of him. "Do this in memory of me."

It is easy for me to forget that everything that I have is from God; like the disciples in the Gospel today I fear that there will not be enough. I fear that the needs of others, my family, friends, and neighbors will ask too much of me. I do not want to think about the needs of strangers or of the needs of so many people around the world. I am not ready to give all that

I have, not to mention the best of what I have, so that others might have life.

But that is exactly what Corpus Christi is about. It is a celebration of abundance, the celebration of abundant life offered to us in the Eucharist. At the same time it is a call to share that abundance with others. It is a call to have faith in God's bountifulness and confidence that there will be enough for all.

"Do this in memory of me" is an invitation to recall the Eucharistic presence of Christ and at the same time it is also an invitation to give of ourselves to others just as Jesus does in the Eucharist, without reserve, without holding back—a nice thought but we really need to bring it down to earth. What does this mean in terms of how we live daily? What does the Eucharist call us to in our families and in our work? Does the Eucharist inform our social policies such as health care or immigration? Does the Eucharist urge us to care for and protect the most vulnerable members of our society?

Jesus is present in the Eucharist. His presence calls us to give of ourselves as he gives of himself, completely without reserve. His presence calls us to give the very best of what we have and who we are to both friends and strangers, to both neighbors and visitors. That giving will make the difference for us and the world that we live in. And just like in the Gospel today, after we get over our fear, there will even be twelve great baskets of extras after we all have been satisfied.

Tenth Sunday in Ordinary Time

Anne Termini, former Maryknoll lay missioner

Guatemala

First Kings 17:17–24; Psalm 30:2, 4–6, 11–13;
Galatians 1:11–19; Luke 7:11–17

When the Lord saw her, he had compassion for her and said to her, "Do not weep."   —*Luke 7:13*

If the readings of today were parts in a play, which part would you choose? How many grieving mothers who have lost their children are just hoping they can be the widow in the scriptures? They are longing for God to bring back their loved one, to relieve them of their agony. Perhaps we have met women who've been the other widows, or maybe we ourselves have played the role of the mothers who ask themselves, "Why me, God? Is my faith not strong enough for you to bring back my child? Did I deserve this?"

And then there is the part of Paul, of course, who doesn't immediately respond to God's call. It seems like he has to "think about it." He's that guy who sits on the fence and then gets to be the hero of the story. Are we someone who envies the people in our lives who don't seem to suffer as much as we do?

Theologians, lay people, ordinary people, believers, and nonbelievers have been trying to figure out the meaning of suffering for as long as there has been pain. We can look at it in the abstract, we can ponder it in courses, in retreats, and in quiet prayer, but however I look at it, I choose not to believe that God is willing it on us so that we can understand and love God more. No—suffering is simply painful. The widow did not need to live through the agony of her child dying only to have Elijah revive him—nor did she need to be tested. But her child was revived, and she did rejoice, and her suffering ended. Good did come out of death. That is to be embraced.

The faith of so many I have encountered in my time as a missioner ranks close to those people whose stories are told in the scriptures, yet their losses and suffering continue. In times of loss and grief it is so difficult to believe that death can result in life. Perhaps not so simply as in the scriptures, but with contemplation, time, and prayer, one can see the good things that have happened since the death of a loved one.

Many years ago, as a missioner in rural Guatemala, I worked with a small group of women from a tiny village parish who visited the sick; they called themselves the *visitadoras*. Through a series of leadership workshops we trained the women to respond to their community needs. At our "graduation" I remember Paula, a young lady barely five feet tall proudly holding her small child, Luis, in her arms. Standing next to her was María, childless after four years of marriage.

A few years later when I was visiting the community I stopped in at María's home. There she was, with her beaming husband. In his arms was a beautiful baby girl. Having been there just a few months before, and remembering María's story of how she still was not pregnant, I was puzzled.

María recounted how a few weeks earlier she and the other women in the group visited Paula after her second child, a baby girl, was born. Paula died a week later from an untreated infection. Left with little Luis and a newborn baby girl, Paula's husband made the difficult decision to return with Luis to his family's home in another part of the country. He "gifted" the baby girl to María and her husband.

I will never forget the family photo I took of Maria, her husband, and newly adopted baby, whom they named Lourdes. Their life was the fruit of suffering. It had nothing to do with faith, or lack of faith, or punishment, but it was indeed a gift, and God was present with them through it all.

Eleventh Sunday in Ordinary Time

Sr. Teresa Hougnon, MM

Kenya

Second Samuel 12:7–10, 13; Psalm 32:1–2, 5, 7, 11;
Galatians 2:16, 19–21; Luke 7:36–8:3 or 7:36–50

Then I acknowledged my sin to you, and I did not hide my iniq-
uity . . . and you forgave the guilt of my sin.   *—Psalm 32:5*

Since I entered religious life as a Maryknoll sister, I have lived
in community with women from different cultures from my
own. I cherish this aspect of my life because I have learned so
much about myself in trying to understand others. It is difficult at times, but the joy of recognizing others, being understood by them, and sharing our lives together surpasses the
challenges.

One experience I had in community taught me how to listen to others. In a community meeting one day, another sister
and I had a disagreement. We both wanted the other to see
things our way. She decided to "give in" to me, because I
"never listen" to her anyway, and "in fact, have not listened
at all since we lived together." We realized that we could not
settle our differences in that meeting and agreed to meet
the next day, just the two of us. I really wanted to listen to
her and hear why she felt that way. For the next twenty-four
hours, I prepared myself for our meeting by continually saying to myself, "Just listen," like a mantra. To do this I also
had to set aside any other feelings I had, about the decision
we had made, or whether I felt she listened to me. Those feelings didn't go away, but I had to forget about them for the
moment and just listen to what this sister had to say. When we

met, I listened to her and really heard how she felt, about our previous interactions and my responses to her contributions. I saw myself in a new way, and I saw how I could change my behavior in order to really listen better. At the end of our time together, she told me that it was the first time she really felt I had listened to her. We didn't resolve all our differences that day, but I gained a valuable insight into my own behavior. For me to set aside my own feelings took humility and faith in our goodness as human beings, faith in our relationship, and faith in God.

Today's readings also talk about humility and faith. In Galatians, we read that we are made just and holy by faith in Christ, not by the observance of the law. Observance of the law is important in Jesus' teachings, but it is always superseded by love of others, which comes out of our faith in Christ. And in Samuel, Nathan tells David he has sinned against God. David listens to Nathan and understands what he has done. He humbles himself and confesses his sin. Upon hearing his confession, Nathan told David that God has forgiven him. He is reconciled to God by admitting his sin, by owning up to what he did wrong. There is still a price to pay, as David is told "the sword shall never depart from your house," but he was forgiven.

Here in Kenya, people are still suffering the effects of post-election violence that took place in 2008. Many are still in camps for internally displaced people. Some individuals need healing from their traumatic experience, and many victims are left without justice. The coalition government, formed during negotiations in February 2008, set out an agenda in the National Accord Agreement to end the crisis and address long-term issues and possible solutions leading to dialogue and reconciliation. A key part of that agenda is the Truth, Justice, and Reconciliation Commission (TJRC), mandated to look at human rights violations between 1963 and 2008. Similar commissions have been mandated in over thirty countries in the past thirty years, shaped according to the local situation, understanding, and need.

As I have listened to the Kenyan people and participated in several discussions around the TJRC Act, as it is known here, I have heard much more emphasis placed on justice than on reconciliation. This emphasis is also reflected in the makeup of the commission, as seven of the commissioners are lawyers. There is not one religious leader on the commission. Where possible, I have advocated for a focus on reconciliation and the unique role of the Catholic Church in such a process.

In our ministry, we sit with small groups of Kenyans from different ethnic backgrounds, different faiths, or different economic classes and facilitate conversations about their experience, their hopes, and their dreams. In these groups, some have found healing by telling their stories and being heard. Others have been able to confess, with humility, their part in the postelection violence, and this also is healing. They hear each other and understand that despite their differences, they are brothers and sisters. This is about restoring relationships, reconciliation. We go about it in a small way, and it takes time.

In today's Gospel reading, Jesus joins Simon, a Pharisee, at his house for dinner. The Pharisee understands the importance of following the law, and knows himself to be a good person for observing the law. Simon also knows that the woman who has come to wash Jesus' feet with her tears is a sinner. He says to himself, "If this man were a prophet, he would have known who and what kind of woman this is who is touching him." Jesus knew well that she was a loving, faith-filled woman. And it was because of her faith and the love she extended to Jesus that her sins were forgiven.

The Pharisee, caught up in following the law, being a "good person," did no more than was required of him to seat his guest at his table, no water for his feet, no kiss, no oil for his head. These things came from the one who had sinned more, and loved more. These things are about relationship. She humbled herself to come into the dinner party, and acted out of love.

May we love much.

Twelfth Sunday in Ordinary Time

Fr. Steve Judd, MM

Bolivia

Zechariah 12:10–11; 13:1; Psalm 62; Galatians 3:26–29;
Luke 9:18–24

*Then he said to them all, "If any want to become my followers,
let them deny themselves and take up their cross daily and follow
me. For those who want to save their life will lose it, and those
who lose their life for my sake will save it."*   —Luke 9:23–24

For the past several years I have had the privilege of participating in pilgrimages to the remote eastern provinces of eastern Bolivia, the site of what were once the Jesuit mission reductions, which flourished until the Jesuits were expelled from Latin America in 1767. Most of us are familiar with the celebrated movie *The Mission*, which popularized a little-known story of an era of peaceful evangelization that brought together the Renaissance-era European Jesuit missioners to encounter the indigenous peoples of vast areas in Brazil, Argentina, Paraguay, and Bolivia. This compelling film gave us indelible images of peace-loving peoples caught in the battle between avaricious Spanish and Portuguese frontier settlers for ownership of the land and the enslavement of these nomadic peoples. The movie documents the violent demise of this utopian experiment, ending with a child shown on the screen playing a haunting melody on a flute.

One would not expect to discover much that remains of these largely abandoned territories and mission towns of that earlier period. But a pleasant surprise is in store for those who journey there. Instead of the ruins of the reductions that one finds in Paraguay, Brazil, and Argentina, here in the low-lands of Bolivia the visitor glimpses the splendor of restored mission-style churches and, more importantly, faith-filled communities of the descendants of the tribal peoples the first Jesuit missioners encountered.

Even after centuries of only sporadic evangelization efforts, indigenous communities thrive in many of the mission com-pounds and churches. Moreover, the baroque music of the Jesuit era has undergone a revival and continues to be played by local youth orchestras and choirs in magnificent concerts in packed churches. In many ways that scene of a young child playing the flute is repeated every day in the constellation of mission towns as a kind of never-ending sequel to *The Mission* and a reminder that all of humanity has been gifted by the heritage of this blessed encounter.

During these frequent visits I am often challenged to wres-tle with the same question that Jesus posed to his disciples in today's Gospel: "Who do the crowds say that I am?" When I am among people who have been subjected to oppression and social and economic exclusion for so many years by a suc-cession of landowners, loggers, and corrupt officials not very different from the first outside settlers, I wonder how it is they understand their relationship with Jesus.

When I look around at the congregations assembled in the churches, the answer comes through in their rapt and reverent attention at the Mass, in the stirring musical compositions, and in the gentleness that permeates the whole environment. If asked the same question they would not be able to present theological and Christological arguments of who Jesus is for them, but their quiet and solemn manner speaks volumes that Jesus is very much alive for them in the solitude of these remote frontier outposts. They give expression to that presence of the

Risen Lord in new and creative musical compositions that draw upon the Baroque tradition as well as the wellsprings of their own rich indigenous cultural heritage.

In contemplating these portraits and human mosaics, especially in the voices of the children's choirs, St. Paul's words in the second reading, from Galatians (3:26–29), take on new and profound meaning, namely, of being united as children in Christ. All of us become clothed in Christ in that setting, and the normal distinctions between people evaporate in this faraway place. One feels like no other time before the powerful truth of Paul's words: "There is no longer Jew or Greek, there is no longer slave or free, there is no longer male and female." Here the barriers between peoples of such diverse backgrounds and national origins break down. In such a place we can take ownership, perhaps for the first time, of the common heritage we have in Christ. As heirs across real and artificial frontiers we can claim a new vision of the human family in the utopia of a more just and equitable world.

This is the same vision that many indigenous people in Latin America speak about today that is captured in the phrase *vivir bien,* translated into English as the capacity "to live well"—in harmony with each other and all of Creation. It means to have enough of life's basic necessities and to be able to share whatever bounty Earth gives us. The phrase does not mean to "live better" or beyond our means as if in the competitive world we all know so well; nor does it mean doing whatever it takes to get ahead. The gentle and hospitable people of this corner of Bolivia "evangelize" us to these greater and more meaningful truths that "another world is possible." By that they echo the spirit of the readings of this Sunday that Jesus is alive in the silent and the soft tones of a melodious witness of people who stir our consciences and awaken our imaginations to the wonder of a Creator God.

The image of the little child playing the flute at the end of *The Mission* can be found in Bolivia and almost anywhere in our world if only we take to heart new ways of relating to each other and to Creation. We need only to pause a moment in our hurried lives and take the time to discover that child proclaiming and urging us to *vivir bien*.

Thirteenth Sunday in Ordinary Time

Liz Mach, Maryknoll lay missioner

Tanzania

First Kings 19:16–21; Psalm 16:1–2, 5, 7–11;
Galatians 5:1, 13–18; Luke 9:51–62

*No one who puts a hand to the plow and looks back is fit for the
kingdom of God.*   —*Luke 9:62*

In the agrarian society in northwestern Tanzania along Lake
Victoria where I live, the plow, the land, and the oxen, all spoken about in today's readings, are a part of the fabric of life.
We depend on the fresh "fruits of the earth" to eat and the
rain from heaven to drink.

The back-breaking work of cultivating the land by hand
is the everyday reality of life here. We live in harmony with
the seasons. We embrace the weeks of heavy rains that water
our crops so they can be brought to harvest and the weeks
filled with dry, dusty, windy days that allow folks the time to
rebuild broken-down and washed-away mud brick homes and
dirt roads. Cattle munch the grass near rivers; the water from
streams is used for bathing, cooking, and drinking. Our neighbors depend on nature's goodness to eke out a living. We have
come to know how disturbances in rainy or dry weather can
disrupt a delicate harmony and cause great havoc. In some
cases, imbalances come not from nature, but from human-
made ecological damage in the name of acquiring something
that others feel they "need."

In our diocese of Musoma we are confronted by the mining
of newly found gold deposits in the area. Toxic metals that are
used to extract gold from ore leach into the ground. These

toxins often pollute local water systems. Water is contaminated—the same water used for bathing, cooking, and drinking—and the tainted soil becomes unfit for crop production. We witness the negative effects on people living close to these poisonous accidental spills: cattle die, human skin disease escalates, and spontaneous abortions in pregnant women climb.

But what rights of protest do our neighbors have against these powerful outside forces? The silent majority of people who rely on clean water and healthy soil for their survival are often without rights as contracts and money exchanges take place at a level well beyond their reach.

Closer to home, the lives of those who surround the mine are directly affected by our own need for metals for the manufacture of components used in a wide range of electronic products and equipment, including computers, telephones, cellular phones, and home appliances. We don't often make the connection between our needs and the lives of a simple farmer tilling the land in a far-off land. But the connection is there, and we have the responsibility to remember these folks and to weigh our own choices with how they affect the lives of others.

The call to be Christians, to put our hand to the plow and to follow Jesus, is tougher in today's interconnected global context. Today's readings ask us to respond to Jesus' Gospel request to "Follow me." In the second reading we are reminded that "you shall love your neighbor as yourself." It seems fitting then to remember our neighbor in the choices we make, for in truth we love them in the same way we love ourselves. Simply put, Jesus asks us to make conscious decisions that satisfy not only our own needs but the needs of our brothers and sisters and the earth in which we live.

We have the responsibility to remember and to take into account Earth's needs as well—not only because we rely on soil, water, and all of Earth's life-giving matter to fulfill our own needs, but also because we have been charged with the responsibility of protecting and respect Earth as God's great work of beauty. As we put our hand to the plow today and go forth, we remember that we are called to be faithful witnesses to the Good News of Jesus. That Good News is reflected in the choices we make for ourselves, our Earth, and our brothers and sisters.

Fourteenth Sunday in Ordinary Time

Tim O'Connell, former Maryknoll lay missioner

El Salvador

Isaiah 66:10–14; Psalm 66:1–7, 16, 20; Galatians 6:14–18;
Luke 10:1–12, 17–20 or 10:1–9

*After this the Lord appointed seventy others and sent them on
ahead of him in pairs to every town and place where he himself
intended to go.* —Luke 10:1

Jesus sent his disciples in pairs to prepare the way for him. As
Luke tells us, they traveled light: "Carry no purse, no bag,
no sandals." Their mission was sacred and directed by Jesus
himself.

For millennia, followers have been sent to share the Good
News with others. When my wife, Ellen, and I went to mission
with Maryknoll it was different than it was for the seventy of
today's Gospel. For one thing, we had stuff, including extra
sandals, and even a laptop.

Despite these differences and many others, some aspects of
mission never change. Fortified by faith we left our comfort
zones to share the Good News. We encountered myriads of
people, some more willing than others to allow us into their
lives. More often than not we received a warm welcome and
abundant hospitality. We ate and drank what was offered, even
when we knew we might fall ill from microscopic bugs. It was
a small price for the opportunity to grow in communion with
the people of Latin America.

During our time in El Salvador it was clear that God was
already there. Our mission became that of doing whatever God
might ask of us in a given day. We tried to build relationships

with people hoping to create sacred space into which the Holy Spirit might enter and transform us all.

One man who helped transform me is Hector, a husband, father, and friend, whose work requires a strong body that can work long hours. In his precious free time, Hector has volunteered as a catechist and taught marriage preparation classes with his wife, Sylvia. He, Sylvia, and some friends have sung and prayed with women in prison and fed homeless people at night in the streets of San Salvador. Hector is driven by faith and filled with joy. He is a man inspired by Jesus, doing all he can to share his love. Hector continues to inspire me to live a more "discipled" life.

Today I work in Hispanic ministry outside of Philadelphia, assisting people from Latin America who have come in search of opportunity. Like the disciples, they must knock on doors uncertain if they will find people of peace or hostility. It is a tremendous act of faith and sometimes desperation.

While our country as a whole may not welcome them, many people do. Each day I'm privileged to witness the compassion of clergy, religious, and lay people of many faiths opening their doors wide to accompany and assist these neighbors in their daily struggles and celebrations.

As I learned in El Salvador, this is never a one-way street. I receive so much from those to whom I minister. Their faith in the face of poverty and exploitation humbles me. Their hospitality and gratitude overwhelm me. And their sense of God's presence in daily life challenges me.

These modern-day disciples come to this country seeking a living wage to sustain their families. They are the workers packing meat, picking lettuce, scrubbing toilets, and building homes, often for less than minimum wage. Their labor makes our lifestyle possible.

These people arrive with dignity but suffer from vulnerability and fear. With their presence, they invite us to follow Jesus, live the Word, and work with them to build the Kingdom. How are we responding to this invitation?

Henri Nouwen writes, "The suffering Christ of North America and the suffering Christ of South America are one. They cannot be separated or divided without reenacting the crucifixion over and over again."

As Catholics we are called to be Resurrection people. But many of us still struggle with the reality of undocumented people among us. Through prayer and action we must find a way to cross psychic borders and transcend the fear that prevents us from welcoming strangers as our sisters and brothers in Christ.

Fifteenth Sunday in Ordinary Time

Fr. John Corcoran, MM

Maryknoll, N.Y.

Deuteronomy 30:10–14; Psalm 69:14, 17, 30–31, 33–34, 36, 37; Colossians 1:15–20; Luke 10:25–37

"Which of these three, do you think, was a neighbor to the man who fell into the hands of the robbers?" He said, "The one who showed him mercy." Jesus said to him, "Go and do likewise."
—*Luke 10:36–37*

Moses often tells the people journeying through the desert that God is not far from them. God is not in some distant place; God is always easy to approach and to talk to. In today's first reading, Moses says that God's very law and commands for us are already in our hearts, not way up in the sky or across a vast sea. This is a powerful message of Moses for all of us: our God is here and now, close at hand and even within our very selves. And God's will for us, God's word and law, are easy to understand and always accessible to each and every one of us. This essential teaching of Moses is brought home to us by Jesus in today's Gospel, perhaps most famous of all stories, that of the Good Samaritan.

Decades ago when I was in Korea struggling to learn the language, the story of the Good Samaritan was in the government sixth-grade reader. Years later, making the same effort to get a little fluent in the Nepali language, the Good Samaritan was in the middle-school reader. These two societies were at that time not Christian or Jewish in any way, but they knew the message of this parable was for everyone.

We are all familiar with the story, so much so that we can miss the essential message of Jesus: We are, all of us, *connected*; we are brothers and sisters in this one world. The Samaritan is an unlikely role model for Jesus and his listeners. The Samaritans, who lived right next to Judea and Jerusalem, were schismatics and heretics despised by true Israelites and corrupters of the true faith—worse than out-and-out pagans. Jesus is driving the message home: we are, *all* of us, brothers and sisters in this world created by the Father. The man who was beaten half to death and robbed of all he had, who was he? A Jew, another Samaritan, a pagan, a rich man, or a poor man? We don't know; all we know is that he was a human being, our brother. And this Samaritan sees his brother and gives to him all the help he can—his time, his money, and his continued love and service.

The priest and the Levite were most likely fervent worshipers of the true God, even in a way "professional" servants of the true Covenant. In fact, going to help this man, who was seemingly already dead, would be a violation of their professional religious duties. Touching the poor beaten man would have made both the Levite and the priest unclean for worship—and they "passed by" on the "other side." They were indeed keeping an important point of the Law, but they were failing in the basic law, the basic relationship all of us have to our human being brothers and sisters in this world.

The walls and divisions and barriers in this world have unfortunately become even wider and higher in our time. Divisions of religion, economic status, race, color of skin, education, language—almost everything. But we are called by Moses and by Jesus in today's parable of the Good Samaritan to embrace humanness first and foremost and overcome every other command or division.

Today let us struggle to walk in the footsteps of this Samaritan, to see with his eyes and be moved with compassion. God indeed is close at hand, in that beaten and robbed man. And God wants of each and every one of us to approach with open hearts and minds as we come to the aid of those desperate fellow human beings we meet on our daily travels.

Sixteenth Sunday in Ordinary Time

Sr. Ann Hayden, MM

Maryknoll, N.Y.

Genesis 18:1–10; Psalm 15:2–5; Colossians 1:24–28;
Luke 10:38–42

*"Martha, Martha, you are worried and distracted by many
things; there is need of only one thing."*   *—Luke 10:41*

These are long, hot days not because of summer but because
we live in intense times of hot-button issues from which there
seems to be no rest.

We are under constant warnings, predictions of danger to
our security from terrorists, melting ice caps, war, and corpo-
rate greed. There is an air of being on constant alert for the
next disaster lurking on the horizon or in the stranger walking toward us across the desert. As we worry about national
security and long for simpler days, we feel less and less secure.
We build so many walls of suspicion to protect ourselves from
the unknown that we spend more time resisting than resting
in the heat of the day like Abram and Sarai did in the shade
of their tent. With our guard up and the doors of our hearts
closed, how can we be pleasantly surprised as they were by
uninvited guests, strangers whom they welcomed unafraid?
Their hospitality was immediate and wholehearted, and they
were blessed with the promise of new life.

Several Maryknoll missioners work tirelessly in Thailand,
responding to the plight of refugees who flee across borders to escape political, ethnic, and domestic violence in
their countries of origin. The immigrants, most of whom are
undocumented, are periodically rounded up by Thai police

and herded into detention centers where they are processed for immediate deportation or held for a review of their case. Maryknollers, working collaboratively with other missionary groups, provide legal and immigration counsel and offer some pastoral and medical care for the detainees, some of whom have spent three years behind bars while their application for refugee status is reviewed. These desperate men and women are lonely for their family and friends. They hunger and thirst not just for more company, food, and water but for recognition and respect as human beings. They long to be treated with dignity and kindness.

The way of compassion and truth is the song of the Psalmist today. Psalm 15 calls us to integrity of relationship that refuses to profit from the difficulties of the other. The plight of displaced and migrating persons is probably the biggest human rights issue around the world today. Immigrants do not want to leave their homes and families but often are faced with the dire choice of leave and live or stay and die in situations of escalating violence or ever worsening poverty. The causes of this global phenomenon are not only local in origin, as many of us would like to believe; they are global, jumping borders at will. The solutions as well need to be both global and local.

St. Paul teaches in today's second reading that all whom he meets are called to receive the message that there is a mystery among us true for each and every generation: all life is sacred and filled with hope. Paul calls us to hold to this wisdom as the mark of maturity in Christ. We are messengers of truth to one another that God's love is for all. We are called by God's love to cross borders for the sake of the truth that Jesus taught— the fullness of life is for all. In God's love there is no room for division into "us" and "them." In God's love there is only *we*.

Today's Gospel from St. Luke is set in the context of discipleship, and Jesus clarifies with Martha that discipleship is often about openness to the unconventional, learning from unfamiliar behavior, exploring new relationships without judgment and embracing our differences with compassion. Finding rest in the heat of today is all about sitting at the feet of the Christ. Peace is difficult to attain if we do not learn to abide in the truth that *we* are *one*. We are called to trust in the wisdom of the Spirit at work in all of creation. This is our way as disciples of Jesus.

Seventeenth Sunday in Ordinary Time

Fr. Michael J. Snyder, MM

Tanzania

Genesis 18:20–32; Psalm 138:1–3, 6–8; Colossians 2:12–14;
Luke 11:1–13

*Then the LORD said, "How great is the outcry against Sodom
and Gomorrah and how very grave their sin! I must go down
and see whether they have done altogether according to the outcry that has come to me; and if not, I will know."*
—Genesis 18:20–21

In our first reading this Sunday, God is ready to destroy the
cities of Sodom and Gomorrah because of the residents' sinful way of life. This should be a wake-up call for each of us
wherever we are. God is not blind to our way of life; rather
God sees everything. I reside in Tanzania, East Africa, one of
the poorest countries in the world. Here, as in so many countries in Latin America, Asia, and Africa, resources are meager.
Everybody wishes for a better life, but the means for obtain-
ing it are few. And so those with influence, those with a bit
of wealth are positioned to benefit from the limited resources
available. And if they are not conscious of the plight of others,
they can amass wealth (homes, vehicles, money) while the
majority suffer in poverty.

Does this sound familiar to you? I wonder where you are living as you read this homily reflection. This situation is not the
exclusive possession of the developing world; even the developed world is full of the children of Sodom and Gomorrah.
You see greed, envy, gluttony, avarice—these are characteristics that have plagued humankind through the centuries. We
see it all around us today and so does God!

In the book of Genesis, Abraham beseeches God not to punish the multitudes for the sins of the few. And so God relents and holds off punishment. But soon afterward it becomes clear that all are guilty, and so the cities of Sodom and Gomorrah are destroyed.

A popular song among Christian young people today comes from the United States, but it is sung even by students at the medical university in Dar es Salaam, where I serve as chaplain. In "Our God Is an Awesome God," the chorus says:

> *Our God is an awesome God.*
> *He reigns from heaven above.*
> *With wisdom, power and love*
> *Our God is an awesome God.*

The verses are very interesting:

> *When he rolls up his sleeves*
> *He ain't just puttin' on the ritz.*
>
> *There's thunder in his footsteps*
> *and lightning in his fists.*
>
> *The Lord wasn't joking*
> *when he kicked 'em out of Eden.*
> *It wasn't for no reason*
> *that he shed his blood. . . .*
>
> *Judgment and wrath*
> *he poured out on Sodom.*
> *Mercy and grace*
> *he gave us at the cross.*
> *I hope that we have not*
> *too quickly forgotten*
> *that our God is an awesome God!*

Our God is indeed an awesome God. He doesn't wish punishment on anyone. In today's Gospel a disciple asks Jesus to teach him how to pray. Jesus begins by saying that first we should address God as our Father. With all the images that this word brings to our minds, what a poignant characteristic to describe God! God is our Father in heaven, a protector, a sustainer, like our natural fathers on earth. Jesus then goes on to explain how God is willing to do anything good for our sake and will deny us nothing that we need. But God depends upon us, we who believe, to be instruments of God's mercy and grace (that he gave us on the cross as the song says) in this world.

As believers, as Christians, we cannot stand back and watch the world become like the Sodom and Gomorrah of the Old Testament. Be it in the United States, be it in Tanzania, or anywhere else in the world, we are called to stand up for justice and to pursue a world where everyone has "enough." God, however, may not need to punish us for our transgressions; unlike Sodom and Gomorrah, we may destroy the world ourselves if we do not protect nature and if we do not protect and preserve each other.

Eighteenth Sunday in Ordinary Time

Fr. John Northrup, MM

Maryknoll, N.Y.

Ecclesiastes 1:2; 2:21–23; Psalm 95:1–2, 6–9;
Colossians 3:1–5, 9–11; Luke 12:13–21

But God said to him, "You fool! This very night your life is be-ing demanded of you. And the things you have prepared, whose will they be?" So it is with those who store up treasures for them-selves but are not rich toward God.   —Luke 12:21

The importance of life is to be "rich in what matters to God." Everything in life is measured by this. A Mexican expression for being rich in the eyes of God is the favorite phrase *rico en corazón* (rich in heart). How blessed to be "rich in heart," yet there are forces in life that can distract us from what God intends for us. One of these is what the second reading calls "the greed that is idolatry."

All of today's readings and so many passages throughout the Bible unmask avarice as the false god that it is. St. Paul in his first letter to Timothy states that "the love of money is a root of all evils" (1 Timothy 6:10).

For several years I lived in Ciudad Juárez, Chihuahua, Mexico, bordering El Paso, Texas. Those of us who lived in Ciudad Júarez were witnesses to the horrors of materialism. Could we not say it has been the primary motivation behind the violence of the drug trade, the kidnappings, and the extor-tions? I have personally known families who have lost spouses, children, and parents to these evils. It is hard to find words to such people to console them. Could it be that the love of money has brought on all this sorrow? What else could it be?

We pray that people will turn from this idolatry and its path of destruction and join those who are moving in the direction of what it means to be truly rich according to the Gospel!

Today's Gospel passage hints that grace will need to be an important part in stepping away from greediness in all its subtle forms. We could put ourselves among those listening to Jesus at the time that the man asked Jesus to be his arbitrator about some inheritance. Prior to this, Jesus had been trying to help his listeners to value God's providence and to find security in divine love. "Are not five sparrows sold for two pennies? Yet not one of them is forgotten in God's sight. But even the hairs of your head are all counted. Do not be afraid; you are of more value than many sparrows" (Luke 12:6–7). After all of these instructions, the man asking help from Jesus is obsessed with material security. His obsession with possessions has made his heart deaf to values that counted. True, the man was seeking justice. Yet avarice can hide behind many things. The parable Jesus relates reveals the illusion of happiness that material wealth seems to promise.

I often wonder about all the pressures that are put upon young men living in Juárez to cross over the threshold into the drug trade. To be a foot soldier in this business carries the tremendous risk of an early death, bringing great sorrow to their families. Maybe some who grow up in certain neighborhoods of the city seem to have no other choice than to become a member of the local gang. If they do not, they may be afraid of the consequences for them and their loved ones. It has seemed at times to be a hopeless situation. I have celebrated funerals of young people while outside the church are the companions of the deceased. I wonder who among them is thinking that they may be the next. Meanwhile, throughout the United States, others are looking for the money that will help them to buy their next supply of drugs. Do they realize at what cost these drugs are being supplied to them?

Although there seems to be no letup of the violence in the city of Juárez, there are seeds and signs of hope. There are people who are amassing the kind of treasure that really matters, such as a group of Juárez citizens who are looking for ways of uniting neighborhoods by providing recreational space for children, creating cottage industries for the unemployed and especially promoting channels of communication among one another. What a worthy way to share one's time, efforts, skills, and financial resources!

Let us continue our celebration with the one who though he was rich, became poor—that we might share in God's generosity and then share that bounty with others.

Nineteenth Sunday in Ordinary Time

Fr. Charles Dittmeier, MM

Cambodia

Wisdom 18:6–9; Psalm 33:1, 12, 18–19, 20–22;
Hebrews 11:1–2, 8–19 or 11:1–2, 8–12;
Luke 12:32–48 or 12:35–40

"Sell your possessions, and give alms. Make purses for yourselves that do not wear out, an unfailing treasure in heaven, where no thief comes near and no moth destroys. For where your treasure is, there your heart will be also."   *—Luke 12:33–34*

Six weeks ago, on the thirteenth Sunday in Ordinary Time, the Gospel told us that Jesus "set his face to go to Jerusalem." In the succeeding weeks, he has been calling disciples to follow him and instructing them.

Last week and this week Luke has Jesus warning his disciples of the influence of the material world and how it can distract them from higher values. Today he advises them to sell what they have and seek purses that do not wear out, treasures that cannot be lost.

That is a caution we also should heed at both the individual level and the level of society. At the individual level, we are bombarded with advertising creating "needs" for all sorts of material goods. For example, ads for bigger, more high-tech televisions constantly confront us. We have gone from one small seven-inch black-and-white TV in the living room to bigger screens to color sets to televisions in every room to wide screens and now to high-definition. At every stage advertisers have convinced us that we are somehow unfulfilled and certainly unhappy without the latest models. We are persuaded to let other priorities go to make sure we are satisfied.

At the level of society, we see the same dynamics. In the pursuit of greater profits and a more pleasurable lifestyle, we have ignored concerns about safety, the environment, human rights, the dignity of people, family values. A focus on rewards for the stockholders and bonuses for executives has led to a worldwide financial crisis, the loss of family homes, huge environmental disasters, and catastrophic weather calamities related to climate change.

Jesus offers an alternative. In the Gospel today, he says not to be afraid because the Father has already given us the kingdom! And that is enough. We do not need to accumulate more and more but can reduce what we have and our reliance on it and even give things away as alms.

The kingdom is not a series of palaces and warehouses where we can get all the material goods we want. Rather it is a different set of values that help us to appreciate what we have and how we use it and that helps us reorder and understand in a different way what we think we need. The kingdom is not one of material riches but of insight and understanding of the fullness of life and love that God offers us.

Too great a reliance on material things, the things of earth, can blind us to this—and to the needs of others. It can isolate us from those around us, and can hinder our growth as spiritual persons and members of God's family.

How do we avoid that? There must be a deeper awareness of ourselves, our brothers and sisters, and all of creation, and how we all relate to each other, and less concern about the material side of life.

But our conditioning is so strong toward material things. We have so much. How can we learn to do without or with less?

All three readings today suggest that faith is the answer and the way. We are conditioned to believe that we need so many material goods because we do not see how we can survive without them. But we can.

Part of the solution is relinquishing some of the control we think we have, some of our independence, some of our sense of mastery of the universe. Natural events like massive floods, earthquakes, hurricanes, and uncontrolled fires should limit our illusions of grandeur and power.

We need to see that we are one part of creation and that we need and depend on all the other parts of creation. We have some power to determine and guide our lives, certainly, but we cannot be like those stewards in today's Gospel who ignore the rights and needs of others and abuse the power and authority that they have been given.

Faith enables us to take on a more humble role and place in the universe. Our faith can help us give up some of our need to control and use the material world because we can rely on our God, who is with us in Jesus.

The Jesuits in Cambodia have a program to retrain amputee farmers for different kinds of labor. One man in a woodcarving program created an Asian-style crucifix with Jesus on a cross of bamboo. And Jesus' leg is blown off. He is an amputee like the woodcarver.

This man got the message of Christianity. We do not need to be in control of everything and possess all goods because our God is with us. God never promises us that there will not be sickness and accidents and floods and wars. God does promise us that Jesus will be with us to get us through our difficulties. This is what faith is all about.

We must place ourselves in the hands of a loving, generous God and learn to appreciate and trust the love God offers us. Then like the Israelites in the first reading and like Sarah and Abraham in the second reading we will find that our doubts and uncertainties are manageable, our greatest fears unfounded, and that God will lead us to the fullness of life here on earth and also in eternity, even if we do not possess all of this world's material goods.

Feast of the Assumption (August 15)

Sr. Peg Kilduff, MM

Peru

Revelation 11:19; 12:1–6, 10; Psalm 45:10–12, 16;
First Corinthians 15:20–26; Luke 1:39–56

A great portent appeared in heaven; a woman clothed with the sun, with the moon under feet, and on her head a crown of twelve stars. —Revelation 12:1

Today Christians gather to celebrate the Assumption, one of the mysteries of the Virgin Mary's life and death. The Gospel takes us to her encounter in solidarity with her cousin Elizabeth that leads her to proclaim a most marvelous song of radical assumption of the power of God favoring the poor and downtrodden: "He has scattered the proud . . . brought down the powerful from their thrones . . . lifted up the lowly; he has filled the hungry with good things."

It leaves one in awe recognizing the vitality and strength of a faith commitment that knows and understands the suffering caused by the structures of power and vested interests, the powerful who seek to amass wealth though corruption, destruction of lands and peoples, those whose answer to conflict is violence, those who stigmatize and persecute people who are different culturally or racially. This is a woman who can be called upon as a sustainer of faith for those who seek justice in the face of great odds.

The reading from the book of Revelation paints an apocalyptic scene where we are faced with an unequal battle between a woman with child and a perverse monster who, although he has conquered a great part of the earth, wants to snatch the child from his mother. This is a story rich in symbolism. The monster is always the imperial power, and the various heads and horns represent the tentacles by which power is maintained, through military control, civil law, economic rules, religious beliefs, or a means of communication. These "monsters" are those who seek to eliminate the Gospel imperative to seek first the reign of love, justice, and truth.

In the woman and child, the fragile Christian communities see themselves depicted. Women and other vulnerable populations all over the world can recognize in this woman a call to courage and faith in times of anguish and fear.

In the Corinthians reading, St. Paul uses an example of the first fruits of the harvest to explain the resurrection of Jesus. Then he tries to clarify that those who live in Christ and die in Christ will also be resurrected in Christ. So Paul affirms that those who accept the message of Jesus as our passion, as our own way of life, will enter into the fullness of life.

Mary's assumption into the definitive embrace of God also speaks of the reverence and respect we Christians have for all matter created as an instrument of the spirit in all of God's creatures.

Today when entire populations living in poverty are so neglected, and their voices go unheeded, when the distribution of wealth in this globalized world ignores the time-honored principles of the church's social doctrine (equal distribution, solidarity, attention to the common good of all peoples), not only the rights but the very lives of the people are sacrificed.

Today's celebration is a call to all of us to remember the radicalism of Mary and her integrity. If we honor her "Magnificat," we need to denounce war as a means to solve problems; deforestation of our woodlands; devastation of our common home; rejection of people seeking entrance into our country. We must look closely at how our country is faring in promoting equality and justice for all. Our engagement lies there.

Twentieth Sunday in Ordinary Time

Joanne Blaney, Maryknoll lay missioner

Brazil

Jeremiah 38:4–6, 8–10; Psalm 40:2–4, 18; Hebrews 12:1–4;
Luke 12:49–53

*So they took Jeremiah and threw him into the cistern of
Malchiah, the king's son, which was in the court of the guard,
letting Jeremiah down by ropes. Now there was no water in the
cistern, but only mud, and Jeremiah sank in the mud.*

—Jeremiah 38:6

I met Aldenor at the Sunday liturgy at the Church of the
Homeless People in São Paulo. His story is a common one
among the more than ten thousand people who live on the
streets in São Paulo. He worked as a bricklayer in Maranhão,
a state in the northern region of Brazil. His wife got sick, and
most of his salary went to pay for her medication and treatment. He was laid off from his job, and after his wife died, he
lost his house. He lived on the street for months with his two
children, who were eventually taken from him. In his words,
"I was at the bottom of the well with no hope. I came to
São Paulo in search of work so that I can eventually get my
children back to live with me. I've been homeless and hungry
living on the streets."

Aldenor's story is similar to Jeremiah's. In the first reading,
we hear that, by the king's order Jeremiah is lowered into a
cistern to die of starvation. Zedekiah, the king, only agreed to
release the prophet because he believed that his death would
cause riots among the starving population of the city, which
the king hoped to avoid. Jeremiah has been called the prophet

of hope and doom. He consistently denounced the evil deeds of the rich and powerful and the consequences of their actions for the majority of people. Jeremiah suffered years in prison but never gave up hope. Overwhelmed by his experience of God's call, he spoke out time and time again against the status quo that keeps so many people in oppression and poverty.

How do we respond to God's call to denounce injustices? How do we speak and work in favor of the 1.4 billion people in our world who live at the survival level of $1.25 (or less) a day and lack basic necessities of food, water, education, healthcare, and shelter? How do we respond to climate change and ecological destruction on our planet?

Our Gospel today is a difficult one to hear. Jesus tells us that he has come to bring fire to the earth. What is this fire about which Jesus speaks? In biblical times, fire was a sign of God's presence and also a symbol of purification and, at times, fear and division. Perhaps a fire needs to be ignited in us so that we may respond to the needs of our brothers and sisters and our suffering planet.

Jesus uses powerful language in speaking about how one household will be divided against another and members of the same family will be divided. If we truly live out Gospel values, there are consequences in our lives, both for the present and the future. When we prioritize getting along with others or external peace ahead of faithfulness to the Word, we fail in kindling the fire of the Spirit. Consumerism, intolerance, and greed are preached by many in our society. Making decisions for Gospel values is divisive. Including the immigrant, the prisoner, and the one different from me may cause conflicts and challenge family and society norms. Yet we remember that we are surrounded by a great cloud of witnesses, who will help us "run with perseverance the race that is set before us" to live out the mission of Jesus.

Aldenor can testify to the words of today's psalm that proclaims the faithfulness of God. "God brought me out of a horrible pit, out of the miry clay and set my feet on a rock, giving me a firm place to stand." Aldenor has found a way to keep faith and hope alive by participating in the church's pastoral program that works with people who are homeless. He has been able to get seasonal work as well as participate in educational workshops and a recycling project that works to stop ecological destruction.

I participate in the Sunday liturgy where men, women, and children who are homeless come to worship and pray together. For many, it is their only community and family. I am always humbled by the generosity of these folks living on the street or in shelters. They consistently share the little they have with others, and their intercessory prayers are usually about the suffering of others in this world, those who are starving, sick, living with war or violence.

With the help of this group, Aldenor is actively working to be reunited with his family. In his words, "I am learning what it really means to have a generous and compassionate heart. I felt so alone and excluded. It was another homeless person who initially reached out to me and brought me here. I thank God for helping me find hope and courage."

Jesus and Jeremiah suffered for their message of inclusion and solidarity. May we be strengthened in our ability to suffer for the sake of others. May the fire of the Divine Spirit truly be kindled in us so that we may have the courage to more actively work for peace and justice in our communities.

Twenty-First Sunday in Ordinary Time

Fr. Daniel McLaughlin, MM

Brazil

Isaiah 66:18–21; Psalm 117:1–2; Hebrews 12:5–7, 11–13;
Luke 13:22–30

*Indeed, some are last who will be first, and some are first who
will be last.*   —*Luke 13:30*

Being here in Brazil these many years, I have become very
appreciative of the method that the people I work with use to
reflect on the readings from scripture for a particular Sunday.
When they meet each week to prepare the celebration of the
Eucharist, one of the first things they do is a reflection on the
readings. They reflect on the readings in the time of Christ
and then they will try to bring these readings into their daily
life.

It is amazing, being here in Brazil, how I am in touch with
the rest of this world. Because of means of mass communication
today, through Internet, computers, TV, radio, newspapers, I
have instant access to what is going on in the world. Most
Brazilians I work with would know about the wars that are
being waged in Afghanistan and Iraq and between Israel and
Palestine. They would know the political differences between
Colombia and Venezuela; the barriers that nations are creating
to limit immigration, including the walls being constructed
along the Mexico–U.S. border; as well as the wall raised up to
separate Israel and Palestine.

In the first reading, verse 18, Isaiah tells us that God will
come to unite all peoples and tongues. And in the last verse
the author tells us that from all corners of the world people

will come together in adoration of the living God. One of the women who helps to prepare our Sunday liturgies said to us, "How many years have passed since this book was written, and yet we seem so far from what Isaiah is telling us. Why is it that over all this time, we seem to be creating even greater distances among one other?"

In today's Gospel, Luke tells us that Jesus, on his way to Jerusalem, visits the towns where the people gather and there teaches them. When someone questioned him about how many will be saved—will it be only a few?—Jesus does not directly answer the question. He states that salvation is universal and is open for all. But to arrive it is necessary to pass through a narrow gate.

It is not enough to say that we sit at the table and eat with Jesus, that we have sat in the plaza and listened to his teaching. It is not enough, Jesus teaches us, that we practice justice: Christ teaches that those who want to pass through this narrow gate must practice justice and have compassion.

In preparing this liturgy for Sunday the people I work with say how necessary it is to respect others, no matter where they were born; to appreciate and protect God's creation, not to throw our litter on the streets; and to take keep our cars in condition so that they do not pollute. Then one of the men in the liturgy group says, if we do these things, then we, as Isaiah wrote, will be those who come from the east, west, north, or south and take our place at the table in the Kingdom of God.

Twenty-Second Sunday in Ordinary Time

Sr. Sia Temu, MM

Maryknoll Sisters Peace Team, Nairobi, Kenya

Sirach 3:17–18, 20, 28–29; Psalm 68:4–7, 10–11;
Hebrews 12:18–19, 22–24; Luke 14:1, 7–14

*For great is the might of the LORD; but by the humble he is
glorified.* —Sirach 3:20

In the first reading we are reminded to behave humbly in
order to find favor with God. Sirach tells us about the power
of humility in everything we do in our life.

These few verses from Sirach bring to mind a story I recently
heard in my ministry. While facilitating small group conversation in Molo, Kenya, a place that was very much affected
by the postelection violence in 2007 and 2008, a participant
shared how much he was affected by the violence. He happens to be a member of the minority ethnic group in this area.
Those from the majority ethnic group believe that they are the
ones who have the right to occupy the land in this place and
that the rest have to go back to where they originated.

According to this participant, he moved to this area more
than forty-five years ago and bought a piece of land where
he lived with his family. For the most part they enjoyed the
peace and harmony of living as Kenyans with their neighbors.
There was no such thing as tribalism before the first multi-
party election held in 1992. Only then did he start experiencing the turmoil of being different from others. Even then, he
recalled, it was not as bad as it was during the presidential
election of 2007–8. This time around he was evicted from his
house and severely beaten by people he did not know. They

took everything he had and destroyed his property. The same neighbors who used to come and fetch water from his place destroyed the well and threw dirt in it, to ensure that it could not be used anymore.

He said they thought he was dying when they left him after the beating. As they were beating him, he was praying to God to protect him from their harm. He had a great hope and faith in God's power, so he was very sure that God would never leave him. When they had all left him, he slowly got himself up and started walking. He went to the hospital where he was checked and told that he had no broken bones, only bruises and muscle pains.

After he recovered he went to live in an IDP (internally displaced people) camp. Once there was relative peace and calm on the ground he decided to go back to his place, put up a tent, and sleep there. Again at night some unknown people came and dragged him out of his tent and beat him. Again he left for a while only to return after a while—this time with hope and trust that things would be okay. He started rebuilding his place again. He dug another well where he could collect some rainwater. His neighbors came back again as usual to ask for water from his place. He was humble enough to welcome them and to give them water.

One day he recognized one of his cows among the animals that his neighbor was now keeping. Humbly and courageously he went in and asked his neighbor how they could share the fruit of this cow. Realizing that they both needed the cow's milk, he said to his neighbor, "What I want is a good relationship with you. Now that this cow has a calf, you should choose whether you want to give me the calf and you remain with the mother or give me the mother and remain with the calf." The neighbor said that in his tradition it would be good for the man to take the calf and the neighbor remain with the mother. It was that simple and they still relate with each other well without any resentment.

As we read from Hebrews 12:22–24, "You have come to Mount Zion and to the city of the living God, the heavenly Jerusalem, and to innumerable angels in festal gathering, and to the assembly of the firstborn who are enrolled in heaven, and to God the judge of all, and to the spirits of the righteous made perfect." The man was aware of the interconnectedness among neighbors. That's why he was not proud but humble enough to say thank you very much to his neighbor for taking care of the cow during the violence. Now they can all share the blessings God has granted. The man said that he knew from the beginning that his neighbors were good people, since they have lived together in harmony for so many years. He was convinced that the atmosphere of violence made them behave contrary to their values and beliefs. They both recognized each other as God's firstborn and realized that they need each other to enjoy the gifts and talents God has entrusted to each one of them.

The Gospel echoed the reading from Sirach by reminding us how we should share whatever we have with the poor and the less fortunate ones, especially those who cannot repay us. I recall many of the stories I heard during the postelection violence here in Kenya, how people of good will were able to help the victims of violence regardless of their ethnic background. There were donations made everywhere to help the IDPs. Many people volunteered their service without expectation of being paid back.

Let us be reminded to humble ourselves, to take care of one another especially those most in need, and to remember God has many ways of paying us back.

Twenty-Third Sunday in Ordinary Time

Fr. John Barth, MM

Cambodia

Wisdom 9:13–18; Psalm 90:3–6, 12–13, 14–17;
Philemon 1:9–10, 12–17; Luke 14:25–33

"Whoever does not carry the cross and follow me cannot be my disciple."   *—Luke 14:27*

Zeal for Your House is the name of a book written by one of the early Maryknoll priests and founders of the Society, Bishop James E. Walsh. He had gone to China in 1918 with three other pioneers from the new Maryknoll seminary in New York. He worked among people who never heard the Gospels.

"Zeal" is a word we do not hear much these days. According to my dictionary it means: "Enthusiastic devotion to a cause, ideal, or goal and tireless diligence in its furtherance. See synonyms at passion."

In today's Gospel from Luke 14 we hear Jesus relating to the multitudes of people that following him, in the long run, will not be so easy: "Whoever comes to me and does not hate father and mother . . . and even life itself, cannot be my disciple" (Luke 14:26). What Jesus describes is real, enthusiastic devotion to a cause, ideal, or goal, and tireless diligence in its furtherance. Synonyms would likely begin at "passion." Some people after reading this verse would add to the list of synonyms: "*See*: crazy."

Indeed, a multitude followed Jesus in the final months of his journeys in and out of Galilee and Jerusalem. Many hoped for a cure, others for words of wisdom to calm a troubled heart, still others felt ill will toward Jesus. Even at the end his trusted disciples loved their own lives so much that they dropped away from his side when the going got tough.

Being a Catholic priest from the United States working in Southeast Asia I've met many Asians who are interested in Christianity and admire Jesus and his teachings. Few choose to commit themselves through the sacrament of baptism. For some it can, as Jesus relates, cause division in families that do not share the same enthusiasm for a faith other than Buddhism.

I am reminded of a story of "The Rabbit" told by Tim Zingale: One day a young man visited the home of an old man who never missed going to church on Sunday, ever. The old man was sitting on the porch with his dog stretched out before him taking in a beautiful sunset. The young man posed this question: "Why is it that most Christians zealously chase after God during the first year or two after their conversion, but then fall into a complacent ritual of attending church only during holidays or when convenient? People see a faith in you that they do not see in others. What makes you so different?"

The old man smiled and replied, "Let me tell you a story: One day I was sitting here quietly in the sun with my dog. Suddenly a large white rabbit ran across in front of us. Well, my dog jumped up and took off after that big rabbit. With great passion he chased the rabbit over the hills. Soon other dogs joined him, attracted by his barking. What a sight it was, as the pack of dogs ran barking across the creeks, up stony embankments, and through thickets and thorns! Gradually, however, one by one, the other dogs dropped out of the pursuit, discouraged by the course and frustrated by the chase. Only my dog continued to hotly pursue the white rabbit. In that story, young man, is the answer to your question."

The young man sat in confused silence. Finally, he asked, "I don't understand. What is the connection between the rabbit chase and the quest for God?"

"You fail to understand," answered the well-seasoned old man, "because you failed to ask why was it that the other dogs ended their chase? The answer to that question is that they had not seen the rabbit. Unless you see the prey, the chase is just too difficult. You will lack the passion and determination necessary to keep up the chase."

Of those few Cambodians I know who do become Christians many eventually "end the chase." The only glimpse of the "rabbit" they will ever get is what they "see" in the lives and faith of those who remain faithful in the pursuit. This calls to mind Jesus' parable of the sower's seed that falls along the path or among the thorns.

I find solace in the saying that we are not to follow those who have found the Lord, but rather we are to follow those who still seek him (with zeal). Since Jesus isn't traveling among the paddies and along rivers of Cambodia, it falls to us "crazy rabbits" who have Jesus alive in our hearts to "bark up a storm" (in word and action) among so many who have not yet seen him and heard his voice.

Twenty-Fourth Sunday in Ordinary Time

Christine Perrier, Maryknoll lay missioner

Peru

Exodus 32:7–11, 13–14; Psalm 51:3–4, 12–13, 17, 19;
First Timothy 1:12–17; Luke 15:1–32 or 15:1–10

*"Just so, I tell you, there is joy in the presence of the angels of
God over one sinner who repents."*   —Luke 15:10

In Puno, Peru, recently, Marisol, mother of two young boys, provided refuge in her humble home to another mother with three children who had nowhere to go; her husband repeatedly lands in jail and abuses her when he's "free." Marisol and her husband reflected the unconditional compassion and mercy for this vulnerable and broken woman and her children that our God of Love has for us.

Today's readings speak of God's mercy, but if we enter more profoundly into their wisdom, they invite us to be challenged and transformed. In the first reading, we hear one part of the long story of the journey of liberation from Egypt to the Promised Land. The Israelites created an idol to worship, hoping that it would lead them onward to the good life.

How many idols we create! Toward how many objects we direct our attention and energy, while turning away from the simple dream of God for our liberation and joy? Idols are seductive, as they try to represent our desires and ideals, but they in fact enslave us in an eternal frustration of unrealized dreams. Worse yet, idols can be projected as all-powerful (as the only thing that matters) or used to control others with fear or guilt.

In Peru, many idols have been created that have much power and control over the people on the margins. Neoliberal policies of the central government place more value in foreign investment of extraction industries than in the livelihood of the people or care of creation. Land is sold for exploitation or "development" without consulting the indigenous peoples who live there, nor with any concern for environmental protection. Only long after the deals have been made in government offices do the people find out about them. Four lots have been approved and sold for gas exploration in Lake Titicaca; 40 percent of Peruvian land is granted as concessions to mining companies, the majority in indigenous regions with extremely high levels of poverty; and a contract with Brazil opens the doors for the construction of a massive hydroelectric dam that will exterminate forty communities and damage the biodiversity in the region.

Rivers and soils are contaminated by gas and mining companies without any controls, destroying the already fragile ecosystems and food sources of people who have no alternatives. As a result, the majority of social conflicts in the area are due to environmental issues and extraction industries that use their power to threaten and control. The government has criminalized social protest, specifically of indigenous peoples trying to preserve their land and life. At the same time, masses of people living in poverty are lured by the prospect of quick money to enter the mining industry, risking harsh conditions and exploitation for the dream of a better life.

Today's readings remind us that any ideal that is held up as an absolute, including religious doctrine, serves only to exclude and reduce God to an idol. The parables of Jesus are a response to the religious leaders of his time who were criticizing the fact that he freely and intimately accompanied the excluded, those on the margins, and the impure because they did not or could not obey the idol that was created from the "official" understanding of the law. How common it is today to hear religious discourse or doctrine transformed into absolute idols that enslave others with violent images of God, rather than imperfect and ever-changing invitations to the freeing mercy of God.

Jesus makes clear that God is not an all-powerful and fear-inducing god. Rather God is Love, who in great compassion and mercy seeks out those who stray and celebrates when we return with humble hearts. This is a God who becomes vulnerable in order to give us the freedom to either choose life or to create idols that lead us away from God. These idols, as Paul tells us, make us arrogant toward others, persecutors of others who are different from us, and blasphemers in worshipping that which destroys instead of that which gives life. Our very freedom can enslave us to our idols.

In contrast, true liberation is found in becoming aware of our false desires and idols, denouncing them, and returning to the original dream of God for us: joy in sharing life with all creation. It is a humble walk of solidarity with our brothers and sisters of every culture and harmony with creation, requiring of us the humility to put more value in what is lost than in what we have and to transform our loss into great joy within the embracing mercy of our God of love. In the midst of today's idols and challenges, we are called to prophetic witness and creative vision.

Twenty-Fifth Sunday in Ordinary Time

Fr. Tom Tiscornia, MM

South Sudan

Amos 8:4–7; Psalm 113:1–2, 4–6, 7–8; First Timothy 2:1–8;
Luke 16:1–13 or 16:10–13

*No slave can serve two masters; for a slave will either hate the
one and love the other, or be devoted to the one and despise the
other. You cannot serve God and wealth.*   —Luke 16:13

"Who will entrust to you the true riches?" With these very
words Jesus is challenging each one of us to be open to the
other, be it neighbor, relative, fellow employee, or even someone of another religion, ethnic group, or culture. Once we can
say yes to this challenge of Jesus, then we can experience an
open door to understanding and even experiencing what the
Kingdom of God is all about.

The manager in today's Gospel from Luke finds his secure
life about to be snatched away from him and come to an end.
As he foresees that he will no longer be able to maintain the
comfortable lifestyle to which he had become accustomed,
fear enters. He chooses to protect his own self-interests, by
once again deceiving the rich man. His future security then
depends on the relationships that he had built with the master's debtors. In other words, in order to live his life in peace,
he had to adjust his life such that his master's debtors would
trust him.

When we experience a lack of trust we live with uncertainty
and even, at times, fear. In many nations where there are distinctions and divisions among religious and ethnic groups

there is a lack of trust. This is surely not what God's King-dom is about. Trust, on the other hand, leads to peace and harmony.

My own experience living for ten years in what is now South Sudan has revealed to me a deep reality of living with trust and without it—especially between Muslims and non-Muslims. Often the trust that Jesus speaks about in the parable is found on the individual level or among members of smaller groups. It can begin with common courtesies like a greeting, a sign of respect, or an offer of some water to quench one's thirst and go forward from there, developing into a true friendship in which there is understanding and dialogue. This is what Jesus means when he says, "If you can trust a person in little things, you can trust that person in greater."

In cases where there is little or no trust then there is the chance of creating enemies—very often leading to great fear and harm to others. The relationship of distrust between two persons or groups of people is against God's plan of creation. We were not created to oppose or oppress others but to live in harmony, and this is possible only when there is trust.

The debtors in today's Gospel seem to have trusted the manager and in the end even the rich man commended him. Is this to say that we should deceive others in order to protect our own self-interests? No one likes to be deceived or made to look like a fool. We are better suited to be totally honest with ourselves and to live every day in peace and harmony with others. The manager surely had a just and understanding side to him, yet it was only when he was threatened that he allowed it to surface and positively influence his relationships—not only with the debtors but with the rich man as well.

In January 2011 the people of South Sudan voted in a ref-erendum to decide if they want to become an independent nation. This referendum was part of an agreement signed in 2006 between the Government of Sudan and the Sudan People's Liberation Movement effectively ending the twenty-two years of war and conflict that cost the lives of over two million people. Also in the agreement was an understanding that north and south would share resources and integrate civil services. This was not really the case. Like in our Gospel today, before the elections the ruling government of the north made small attempts to be more attentive to the situation and needs of the people of the south only in order to win their approval by providing some services which had always been their right, but not freely given. In a sense it is not unlike the manager of today's Gospel who gave the debtors reward in order to win their approval. In the case of Sudan, the level of trust desired by the government of Khartoum came too late because in the 2011 referendum the south decided to secede from the north, creating the country of South Sudan.

In his letter to Timothy, St. Paul urges that petitions, prayers, and intercessions be offered for those in authority so that "we may live a quiet and peaceable life in all godliness and dignity," and God is pleased with this. Let us keep in mind and prayer the people of South Sudan and its leaders so that there may be a truly peaceful and trust-filled and lasting resolution to this conflict, such that in this moment in their history they may know that the Reign of God is made even more manifest in our world.

Twenty-Sixth Sunday in Ordinary Time

Kathy Seib Vargas, former Maryknoll lay missioner

Mexico

Amos 6:1, 4–7; Psalm 146:7–10; First Timothy 6:11–16;
Luke 16:19–31

*The LORD watches over the strangers; he upholds the orphan and
the widow, but the way of the wicked he brings to ruin.*
                                                    —*Psalm 146:9*

This Sunday's readings are loud and clear in terms of clarifying both the attitudes and the tasks of those who would follow Jesus. They are luminous and pertinent to the challenges Jesus addressed in his times as well as for the challenges of our own.

In our times, hope for the future is threatened by scandalous poverty, the exclusion of millions worldwide trying to survive on less than a dollar a day, the unceasing and increasing use of violence to settle conflicts, and the growing likelihood of rendering our precious planet Earth incapable of sustaining life through our neglect or unwillingness to respect and care for her ecosystems. We witness recurring economic crises, obscene arms expenditures and destruction, while neglecting health and educational needs. We see greater frequency and severity of "natural disasters," alienation, addictions, and family disintegration. Modernity promised us a better quality of life, but we see just the opposite: every day humanity moves toward greater unhappiness, loneliness, discrimination, sicknesses, and hunger. In addition to these dire human consequences, we are also moving toward the irreparable destruction of Mother Earth. We have not yet grasped that she can survive quite nicely without us while we mindlessly court our own extinction.

Today's readings provide plenty of good advice on how we are to respond to these realities. The Gospel even assures us that later on there will be an unfathomable abyss between those who have honored justice and truth as described in Psalm 146 and the Epistle of Timothy, on the one hand, and, on the other hand, those who have placed their selfish comfort and greed above the needs of the poor, as did the nameless "rich man" who ignored Lazarus. He is damned not because he deliberately chose to harm Lazarus but because he turned a blind eye to human suffering.

In spite of widespread despair and discouragement and in consonance with Gospel values, we are also witnessing a time of amazing new hope and inspiration emerging from many peoples, particularly the indigenous peoples of the global south, whose ancient wisdom and traditional relationships with each other and Earth are offering us insights and possibilities that might make our survival as a species once again plausible, possible, and even delightful. In Latin America there is a huge groundswell of people and movements looking to promote and encourage *el buen vivir*, roughly translated as "right living" or "living well." It is also happening in Sri Lanka, where it is called "right livelihood," being implemented in over eleven thousand rural communities, based on the teachings of the compassionate Buddha and honoring the same virtues and practices taught by Jesus.

When the indigenous of the Americas speak of "right living" or when the Sri Lankans talk about "right livelihood," they refer to the entire community of beings that inhabit the world, not just humans, going beyond the "common good," which is reduced only to human welfare without regard for the way humans interact with the rest of creation. It is a proposal to preserve the equilibrium and harmony in all that exists. "Right living" is the fullness of life, in harmony with Earth's cycles and seasons, with the cosmos, in equilibrium with all forms of existence and in permanent respect for all. It returns to and embraces the wisdom generated by millennia of human experience that the West has chosen to ignore through building up, believing, and promulgating an inadequate story or understanding of what it means to be human on this planet.

"Right living" is the way of indigenous and traditional rural communities, and it implies first knowing how to live and later how to live with others. It teaches that it is impossible to "live well" when others cannot, or when our way of life harms Earth and the lives of future generations. It understands that the deterioration of one means detriment to all.

Regardless of the intense exploitation of "resources" (minerals, fertile soils, petroleum, gas, and many others) the great majority of people in "developing" countries continue to be poor. This model and exploitative investments have generated inequality, with great opulence for a few, great poverty for most, and horrendous environmental destruction, affecting all. In the face of this competitive and predatory economy—the proposal of "good living" hails the intelligent choice of a communitarian economy; one that respects life and nature, based on the principles of solidarity, reciprocity, complementarity with work, income, and satisfaction of basic needs for all.

In this mindset, according to the revered grandparents and ancient wisdom seekers, life is not about winning or losing; it is about living well, in balance and harmony with others and with the capacities of an incredibly beautiful and precious, but limited, planet. It is a paradigm of plenty, not of scarcity, and its basic tenet is "that we all go forward together, that no one get left behind, that all have everything and that no one be left out" (paraphrased from the Mayan *Popol Vuh*). In this proposal of a communitarian economy, when harmony and balance are broken, the tragic consequences affect everyone. If one gains and another loses, in fact all of us have lost.

The official teaching of the Catholic Church at the Second Vatican Council proclaimed that "God is present and active in all human societies." These initiatives from the "poor" of the global south are true guideposts for our times. The job of the Christian therefore is to be open to God's activity guided by the light of the Holy Spirit, to recognize the truth and beauty of the ancient traditions that are in fact offering a tremendous surge of hope for humanity and the Earth, if only we abandon our indifference and the hardness of our hearts. We are being called to embrace this life-giving worldview, so generously saved, reverenced, and now offered once again by the "poor" of the world.

In *Gaudium et Spes*, the church also reinforces the same message: "In our times a special obligation binds us to make ourselves the neighbor of every person without exception and of actively helping him [or her] when he [or she] comes across our path, whether an old person abandoned by all, a foreign laborer unjustly looked down upon, a refugee, or a hungry person who disturbs our conscience by recalling the voice of the Lord: 'Just as you did it to one of the least of these who are members of my family, you did it to me'" (Matthew 25:40).

Twenty-Seventh Sunday in Ordinary Time

Fr. John McAuley, MM

Maryknoll, N.Y.

Habakkuk 1:2–3; 2:2–4; Psalm 95:1–2, 6–9;
Second Timothy 1:6–8, 13–14; Luke 17:5–10

But the righteous live by their faith. —Habakkuk 2:4

I first entered Sierra Leone in 1995 with Religions for Peace, at a time when the civil war was still raging in the country. Religions for Peace, an international inter-religious NGO with status in the United Nations Economic and Social Council, was invited by the religious communities in Sierra Leone to assist them in an initial formal engagement of one another. Throughout the country, Animist, Christian, and Muslim towns were being victimized and destroyed by rebel groups who embraced a policy of terror and nihilism. With a central government weakened by corruption related to the blood diamond trade, the religious communities believed that their only defense against relentless maiming and killing was a united stand against the rebels and a united moral voice with which to engage the government and the international community. Their faith-engendered respect for threatened lives was the catalyst that first brought them together.

> *For God did not give us a spirit of cowardice, but rather*
> *a spirit of power and of love and of self-discipline.*
> (2 Timothy 1:7)

The first and most enduring difficulty that the religious communities encountered in coming together was the resistance by third parties to the religious communities' engaging one another within the country. Local politicians often were able to take advantage of seminal distrust among religious groups to build a political base of support and power within single groups. International actors, including third-party states, were also interested in exploiting religious differences within Sierra Leone to build and maintain spheres of economic, political, and military influence. Still, fortified by the partnership of the international and regional structure of religious communities found within Religions for Peace, the religious communities within Sierra Leone pressed forward and formed the Inter-religious Council of Sierra Leone. The council soon took as its first task to address the causes and effects of the civil war symbolized at its worst by the recruitment of child soldiers, and by the ensuing violence perpetrated by them. In cooperation with UNICEF (United Nations Children's Fund), the council began the establishment of safe havens and homes that could offer rehabilitation and transition for child soldiers and also for their female counterparts, "camp followers."

If you had faith the size of a mustard seed, you could say to this mulberry tree, "Be uprooted and planted in the sea," and it would obey you. (Luke 17:6)

A simple act of faith in 1995 that they were being called to give common witness against a long-term, increasingly violent, and chaotic civil war, was followed by a common effort initiated in 1997 to themselves address one of the most pernicious effects of that war, the large number of child soldiers. By the year 1999 the Inter-religious Council of Sierra Leone found itself seated with other regional and international intergovernmental partners as go-betweens and conveners of representatives from the national government and rebel leadership to begin a process of cease-fire, disarmament, and tribunal justice. After decades of a seeming intractable conflict, in five short years the religious communities, acting in concert, transformed their role in society from that of victims to that of peace brokers for the entire nation.

In the United States we are in a period when worldwide there has been a great ongoing loss of life since September 11, 2001, aggravated by subsequent economic shifts that have engendered more uncertainty and dis-ease in our society. Openness to and welcome of those who are significantly different culturally, religiously, and ethnically from longer established social groups is being increasingly challenged. Physical walls are being erected, legislation is being passed, and challenges are being raised about the place in the public square to be given these latecomers, such as we witnessed in the mosque debate in New York in 2010. Unaddressed, these tensions and perceived differences could serve as potential vectors of power and influence for some at the expense of the whole. It may yet be the place of the religious communities to come together in a new way in this country as they did in Sierra Leone to reverse trends that threaten the fabric of social life and the actual lives of individuals, and to re-broker the peace for which we so yearn.

Twenty-Eighth Sunday in Ordinary Time

Kathleen McNeely, former Maryknoll lay missioner

Maryknoll Office for Global Concerns

Second Kings 5:14–17; Psalm 98:1–4; Second Timothy 2:8–13;
Luke 17:11–19

*On the way to Jerusalem Jesus was going through the region
between Samaria and Galilee. As he entered a village ten lepers
approached him. Keeping their distance, they called out, saying,
"Jesus, Master, have mercy on us!"*   *—Luke 17:11–12*

It always amazes me how Jesus seems to turn things upside
down, and in the unexpected twists Jesus teaches us some
important lessons. This is true in today's Gospel from Luke.
After being healed, only one leper out of ten, a Samaritan,
returns to Jesus to offer his gratitude. Jesus offers this one
faithful man as an example of how faith can heal and save us.
The majority of Jesus' followers were Jews, and in this instance
Jesus shows that the non-Jew demonstrated more faithfulness
than the other nine (presumably Jewish) healed lepers who did
not return to offer thanks.

I was a Spanish major in college and spoke and read Spanish
fluently throughout my graduate studies in theology. Shortly
after graduating with my degree, I found myself in the office
of a "head-hunter"—a person who helps place people in both
permanent and temporary jobs. I was looking for a short-term
temporary job in the Boston area, since my heart was set on
living and working in Latin America.

When I told her my plan, she was shocked and said, "Why
would you want to live there?" She said it was hot and dirty
and there were too many flies! She was more diplomatic than

many people confronted with a young person's deviation from the "American dream." But her basic assumption was that I was a lot more like her than I knew and that I would not be comfortable living in a less-industrialized country—because she wouldn't tolerate the heat, the dust, and the flies. She tried to persuade me to look at some more permanent and lucratively paying positions in Boston.

As I left the office, I told her I did not think she could help me; I really wanted something temporary until I found my way to Latin America. She called me two days later and told me she found a "fantastic" position for me in Costa Rica with a U.S. company that sold razor blades and personal hygiene products. Here she was again, with her assumption that I would like what she liked. I told her I was not her woman—I imagined that working for a U.S. company overseas would not get me out into the world I wanted to experience.

I remember questioning her assumptions and becoming hyper-alert when people I encountered said things like "people like us." It clued me in to listen very closely to the assumptions people imagined I shared with them. In fact, I had turned her belief system upside down because instead of wanting to make lots of money while doing international business, I wanted to be stretched beyond my national borders and to understand the joys, challenges, and cultural realities of more marginalized people living in less-industrialized countries.

In the years since the terrorist attacks of September 11, 2001, I find that many people in the United States have continued to make a lot of assumptions about who is like "us" and who is not. Every day it seems that the Department of Homeland Security is given more power and authority to keep us U.S. citizens from having any encounter with "the other," or "them" within our borders. There is an assumption that all of us are basically the same and that we will all feel more secure if we can just keep all of the "foreigners" out.

For the Jews of Jesus' time, Samaritans were the "other"; they were "foreigners" and despised by the Jews. In the healing encounter and in the story of the Good Samaritan, also in Luke's Gospel, Jesus teaches his followers that the most reviled individual—the most totally "them" can exhibit moral and spiritual behavior superior to that of the Jews—the "us" of his time.

Reflecting on this point that Jesus is making, the words from Second Timothy carry new meaning: "the word of God is not chained." It seems that Jesus intended his teaching to reach everyone, or at least those with "ears to hear" (Luke 8:8). He demonstrates this inclusiveness with the characters he chooses for his encounters and his stories—many times they were people who were considered "them" living far outside the comfortable realm of "us." He did not exclude any one community of people and sets an example for his listeners to begin to see people they considered "them" with new eyes.

When I left Boston my heart led me to Nicaragua and later to Guatemala where for a total of six years I shared the joys, sorrows, challenges, and victories of life with people who did not dress like me, talk like me, or look like me, in any way. And yes, there were flies! I went to Nicaragua at a time when U.S. policy was in direct opposition to that of the Nicaraguan government. Nicaraguans were very much considered "them." In living there, I think I was directly imitating Jesus' example from today's Gospel, for he too was traveling in foreign territory—through Samaria and Galilee on his way to Jerusalem. He was actually seeking encounters with Samaritans and others that his followers considered "them."

While living and working among Nicaraguan and Guatemalan communities, I think I found what Jesus was trying to teach that day the lepers walked up to him begging for healing. Instead of fearing a world beyond my borders, I reached out and touched it by immersing myself in it with curiosity and trust. Instead of trying to control and change all the newness I encountered, I allowed myself to watch and to learn and to celebrate the gifts of diversity, hospitality, a deep respect for the natural world, and a sense of gratitude like I had never encountered before.

In the United States I had come to find people desperately trying to control their experiences, planning every minute of every day and designing their lives to let some people in and to exclude others. In Central America I found people whose first instinct was to trust and let God take care of much of their day. They prayed constantly and about everything. "God willing" accompanied every wish to follow through on a commitment. And "thanks be to God" was uttered each and every time they recognized a blessing, including food on the table, the beauty of nature, good health, and the safety of family members. Not unlike the grateful leper, they seemed to live their lives very in touch with the source of all gifts, all healing, and all salvation; they recognized that God grounded their entire being, and for that they constantly gave thanks to God.

If I am ever asked how to best ensure homeland security (I keep waiting for someone to ask) I would have to echo Albert Einstein in saying "no problem can be solved from the same consciousness that created it. We must learn to see the world anew." This seems to be the point of Jesus' turning things upside down for his listener, offering them a chance to see "the other" anew, to embrace diversity rather than fear it and to look to the other as a source of wisdom.

Twenty-Ninth Sunday in Ordinary Time

Fr. Thomas J. Marti, MM

Phillippines

Exodus 17:8–13; Psalm 12: 1–8; Second Timothy 3:14–4:2;
Luke 18:1–8

"And will not God grant justice to his chosen ones who cry to him day and night? Will he delay long in helping them? I tell you, he will quickly grant justice to them. And yet, when the Son of Man comes, will he find faith on earth?" —Luke 18:7–8

The readings for today's liturgy make clear to us, people of faith, the need for persevering and patient prayer and action in bearing witness to the Kingdom of God.

I would like to reflect with you on these values in the context of the serious ecological challenges facing the world today. No less than Pope Benedict XVI has sounded the alarm with regard to rapid global warming and the catastrophic consequences if action is not taken. As people of faith we are morally compelled to respond positively to such challenges as our part in proclaiming and living the Kingdom of God.

I initially became concretely aware of the sin of environmental exploitation while serving as a missioner in the Philippines. I observed firsthand massive deforestation on the island of Mindanao where I served for over ten years. Much of this was due to illegal logging. Most of the timber was simply shipped out in its raw form, mostly to Japan. Most of it was not even processed in the Philippines. Large tracts of mountainous land were left denuded. Landless farmers would then move in and try to eke out a living. Because of the lack of proper tilling methods, vast areas of this once lush land became eroded and virtually useless. Massive floods have occurred, sometimes accompanied by landslides, oftentimes caused by deforestation, resulting in great loss to both life and property.

The unfolding tragedy does not end there. Because of a combination of greed and corruption, many of the once lush tropical forests in the Philippines have disappeared. One report claimed that of the forest cover that existed in 1945, at the end of World War II, only about 13 percent remained standing thirty years later.

As bad as things have become in the Philippines the situation is not without hope. There has been a growing awareness of the problem. Church groups and others have made significant efforts to sound the alarm and to marshal action.

The Catholic Bishops' Conference of the Philippines issued a warning and a challenge as far back as 1988 in a pastoral letter titled "What Is Happening to Our Beautiful Land?" The Maryknoll Sisters are among church groups that have taken positive action, having organized an ecological retreat and reflection center on the northern island of Luzon.

The bishops challenged members of the church in particular to take action: "Faced with these challenges, where the future of life is at stake, Christian men and women are called to take a stand on the side of life." Reflecting on what has been happening in the Philippines the bishops further stated: "In the light of the Gospel we are convinced that this assault on creation is sinful and contrary to the teachings of our faith."

The challenges we have, my brothers and sisters, relate, of course, not only to the Philippines. The threat to the environment, to creation, is everywhere. It is global. We are all responsible! We should see our call to engagement in the light of our faith in Jesus Christ, realizing that, indeed, our "help comes from the Lord, who made heaven and earth."

In his second letter to Timothy, St. Paul stated: "I solemnly urge you: proclaim the message; be persistent whether the time is favorable or unfavorable; convince, rebuke, and encourage, with the utmost patience in teaching" (4:1–2). Be reminded that we are called to preach, to proclaim the Kingdom of God, not simply in words but by our actions. We are called not just to talk the talk, but to walk the walk.

In the first reading, from Exodus, we have the story of the perseverance of Moses in supporting Joshua in defending Israel. Moses was not able to accomplish his task alone but needed the help of Aaron and Hur. We also must work together, in solidarity with others, in the hope of realizing the values of the Reign of God.

From Jesus' parable in the Gospel we are reminded of the need for perseverance. We have the example of the widow who knew her cause was just and did not give up. We must be persevering in prayer and in action, working in solidarity with others in fulfilling the mission we have received: "Go into all the world and proclaim the good news to the whole creation" (Mark 16:15).

Thirtieth Sunday in Ordinary Time

Fr. Thomas Henehan, MM

Bolivia

Sirach 35:12–14, 16–18; Psalm 34:2–3, 17–19, 23;
Second Timothy 4:6–8, 16–18; Luke 18:9–14

"I tell you . . . all who exalt themselves will be humbled, but all who humble themselves will be exalted."   *—Luke 18:14*

In January 2006, Evo Morales, an Aymara native, was inaugurated as the democratically elected president of Bolivia. It was the first time in the history of this indigenous-majority country that a member of one of the indigenous nations was elected president. The following Sunday, at the Eucharistic celebration of the Aymara community where I lived and worked, I asked the people what they felt at the moment when Evo Morales was installed as president of Bolivia. A frail Aymara woman stood up and said, with solid conviction, that she felt so proud because a fellow humble person like her was now the president.

In Bolivia many of the *mestizo* (mixed race) population have found it is very difficult to accept a native person as their president. Even several members of the church hierarchy voiced their concern after the Morales election. For many he does not speak good Spanish, he does not wear clothes that past presidents wore, and he wants to change a system that has been in place for hundreds of years.

In January 2007, one year after his inauguration, I witnessed here in Cochabamba a violent and bloody encounter between poor native farmers and upper- and middle-class mestizo urban property owners. The motives were many but the hate and discrimination were obvious. On that day, I happened to be walking in the area of the violent encounter and I found myself in the midst of the mestizo property owners carrying baseball bats, clubs, and apparently some pistols. The encounter left three men dead, hundreds of men, women, and children hospitalized, and the entire city traumatized. I could not believe what I witnessed and felt.

I later wrote an article about this brutal clash being, among other things, a pastoral failure of the church. I could easily envision people on both sides of the violence having gone through catechetical programs for baptism, first communion, and marriage. They were graduates of Catholic high schools and even of the Catholic university. Where have we failed to overcome prejudice among ourselves, all created in the image and likeness of God?

In the United States potential Congressional action on immigration reform functions to increase both press coverage and people's actions that promote an isolationist view of the world where those who are different are excluded. The discussions regarding the plans to build a Muslim community center in New York City several blocks from the site of the destroyed World Trade Center revealed a public opinion divided over its attitude towards Muslims and their religion.

Throughout the world and since the beginning of time, accepting the "other" as he or she is has been a challenge. We have been quick to judge the other who is "different." Jesus faced this challenge head-on during his public life. In today's Gospel we read the parable of the Pharisee and the tax collector, two very different persons.

In the time of Jesus, those who visited the Temple were obliged to pay a civil tax, which was not collected directly by the Romans themselves but by the elite and powerful families of the local community. They hired tax collectors who were paid a subsistence wage and who, in turn, systematically pillaged and extorted monies from the poor rural folk who arrived at the Temple. As a result, many of the poor guarded a strong hostility against the tax collectors and often despised them as thieves and as collaborators of the Romans. The image of the tax collector was so negative that it was thought that he was incapable of being forgiven for his sins. He was an easy target for the attacks of the Pharisees because he was poor, socially vulnerable, without honor or dignity, and equivalent to a con artist.

In his prayer, the Pharisee appears centered on himself and what he does. He knows that he is not greedy, dishonest, adulterous, or even like this tax collector. But in fact he does not really know who he is. The parable brings us to realize who he really is, not for what he does, but for what he does not do—relate well with others. The Pharisee actually does more than what is required by the Torah, but his fault is that he looks upon the tax collector and judges him as dishonest, greedy, and a sinner. He is discriminating against him because he is a tax collector. Meanwhile, the tax collector acknowledges who he is by his gesture and his words. He is a sinner and this is the content of his prayer.

The message of the parable is indeed shocking to his audience, those who were convinced of their own righteousness and despised everyone else.

In our world marked with discrimination we are challenged by God speaking to us through the readings of today's liturgy. Our God knows no favorites. Our God hears the cries of the oppressed, the wail of the orphan, and the complaints of the widow (first reading).

Feast of All Saints (November 1)

Fr. Paul Masson, MM

Maryknoll, N.Y., and Mexico

Revelation 7:2–4, 9–14; Psalm 24:1–6; First John 3:1–3; Matthew 5:1–12

See what love the Father has given us, that we should be called children of God; and that is what we are. The reason the world does not know us is that it did not know him. Beloved, we are God's children now; what we will be has not yet been revealed.
—*1 John 3:1–2*

Before moving to Maryknoll, New York, in November 2008, I lived in Ciudad Juárez, Chihuahua, Mexico, for ten years. The memory of the people with whom I worked mingles with the tragic news coming from the border area today as I sit down to write this reflection. Whether it is theologically correct or not, I have been relating the beginning of November with death. Just as November 2, "All Souls' Day," overshadows November 1, "All Saints' Day," I have been thinking of Ciudad Juárez, which has experienced thousands of murders in recent years—over twenty-five hundred murders in 2009 alone. Many people I knew are among the dead. At present the city seems to be engulfed in a culture of death; there is a lot of fear and insecurity, hideous crimes, corruption, and a feeling of despair.

In Ciudad Juárez, the people celebrate the lives of their loved ones who have died. Even though many people have to work in the factories, they will find ways to travel to their home villages. They will visit the cemeteries and clean the graves of their relatives. In their homes, and in the churches, they will prepare altars to remember their loved ones who have died.

Each year, on November 2 a Mass is celebrated along the wall that divides Mexico and the United States. The bishops and community members from Ciudad Juárez and Nuevas Casas Grandes participate on the Mexico side while the bishops and people of El Paso and Las Cruces participate on the other. The intention of the Mass is to pray for the immigrants who died during the year while trying to cross from Mexico into the United States. According to some sources, the number of people immigrating to the United States from Mexico has decreased, but the number of deaths of immigrants has grown.

Today, as we celebrate the feast of All Saints, we give thanks for the love and compassion of Jesus Christ, the Son of God, and recognize that through God's love for us, many of our family members and friends who have died have been called to be Saints. In the Sermon on the Mount, Jesus reveals the road to be followed: the path to sainthood, the path that leads to God's presence:

> Blessed are the poor in spirit . . .
> Blessed are those who mourn . . .
> Blessed are the meek . . .
> Blessed are those who hunger and thirst
> for righteousness . . .
> Blessed are the merciful . . .
> Blessed are the pure in heart . . .
> Blessed are the peacemakers . . .

These are all qualities, ways of life that are accessible to all people. All of us can do this: be poor in spirit, meek, and clean of heart. This is a list of values of the Reign of God, values of a culture of Life, which are in contrast to many of the values of society today: to be poor in spirit, as opposed to being arrogant, self-centered, and cruel; to hunger and thirst for justice, as opposed to being indifferent.

Jesus brings more clarity to the reality of the Reign of God when he states: "Blessed are you when people revile you and persecute you." Suffering, persecution, taking risks, putting your life on the line are all an integral part of the life to which we are called. Through our work in mission, many people in Maryknoll have had the privilege of knowing people who have died in the service of the Reign of God. I worked with a French missionary priest, André Jarlan, who was killed in the protests in Santiago, Chile, in 1986 by the National Police. Two Maryknoll Sisters, Carla Piette and Ita Ford, lived and worked in Chile before going to their deaths in El Salvador in 1980. This reality gives new meaning to the reading from Revelation:

> *After this I looked, and there was a great multitude that no one could count, from every nation, from all tribes and peoples and languages, standing before the throne and before the Lamb, robed in white, with palm branches in their hands. . . . Then one of the elders addressed me saying, "Who are these robed in white, and where did they come from?"*
>
> *I said to him, "Sir, you are the one that knows." Then he said to me, "These are they who have come out of the great ordeal; they have washed their robes and made them white in the blood of the Lamb."*

This year, when the people of Mexico are putting together their altars for the dead, they will be remembering women who have been murdered and left lying in the desert, children who have died without the needed medical care, police officers gunned down by automatic weapons, grandmothers who have died with a broken heart. Among these people, there are many saints.

Thirty-First Sunday in Ordinary Time

Curt and Anita Klueg, Maryknoll lay missioners

Kenya

Wisdom 11:22–12:1; Psalm 145:1–2, 8–11, 13, 14;
Second Thessalonians 1:11–2:2; Luke 19:1–10

When Jesus came to the place, he looked up and said to him, "Zacchaeus, hurry and come down, for I must stay at your house today." . . . Zacchaeus stood there and said to the Lord, "Look, half of my possessions, Lord, I will give to the poor; and if I have defrauded anyone of anything, I will give back four times as much."   —Luke 19:5, 8

During Christmas 2006 our young family was living and working as missioners in Mombasa, Kenya. Some fellow Maryknoll missioners were visiting, and we had bought some fresh ocean fish to cook for dinner. The fish turned out to be not-so-fresh and our dinner was spoiled. We quickly went to the *duka* (a closet-sized food store) along the dirt road next to our house where we bought a few vegetables and shared our unfortunate story. Within a half an hour, the materially poor family who owned the *duka* and lived without electricity or running water showed up at our door with a bowl full of *pilau*, a delightful East African dish of meat, rice, and spices. The hospitality of Kenyans is amazing and was beyond our expectations.

When we arrived as missioners in East Africa, I was expecting some resentment towards white Westerners. After all, the continent has a long history of being exploited for its resources and its people. Most of the national borders in Africa were decided not by Africans but rather by a meeting of colonial powers in Berlin in the 1880s. This paternalistic and exploitative mentality has continued through the present day, as witnessed in recent decades as the CIA became involved in financially backing a coup in Zaire/Congo and as the U.S. military continues to develop its controversial AFRICOM program to train militaries and establish a foothold in the strategically important horn of Africa rather than invest in development.

Far from our feeling resentment, the welcoming spirit of East Africans toward "westerners" surprised us. In language school we remember walking through villages and hearing *karibu* (welcome) from nearly every household. This was not a general "how are you doing?" but rather a genuine invitation into the homes to spend time with people and get to know them. Peter Majura and Thekla were both students at the local high schools in Musoma, Tanzania, where we were placed for language school. Both they and their families invited us to their homes, taught us how to cook traditional foods, shared stories, pictures, and culture. While they generously gave so much, nothing was asked of us but to share our own stories. There is a tradition of washing the hands of guests before any meal. The beautiful ritual is just one example of the importance of welcoming and hospitality to all that come into a home.

The hospitality and generosity demonstrated by the Kenyans and Tanzanians is played out in the Gospel story today; while we play the role of Zacchaeus, they play the role of Jesus. Jesus' followers see Zacchaeus as an exploiter who made his wealth off the backs of the poor. Yet Jesus, sensing his passion and repentance, welcomes Zacchaeus into the fold. But Zacchaeus knows that this newfound faith comes at a cost. He insists that half of his wealth be given to the poor and anyone who has been extorted shall be repaid four-fold! Wow, what a different world we would live in if poor nations were repaid four-fold for the hardships and thievery brought upon them through slavery and exploitation.

Just as Jesus demonstrated his love for Zacchaeus, the Tanzanians and Kenyans we met were able to look past our nationality and embrace us for our desire to accompany them.

This same principle can be applied globally. If we, as a nation, act in the spirit of Zacchaeus, if we drastically reduce our bloated military expenditures ($737 billion in a fiscal year 2011, according to the National Priorities Project) and instead support efforts for peace and development, the world will embrace our passion and kindness in the way that Jesus embraces Zacchaeus. As it did for Zacchaeus our faith demands a change of behavior. Many have praised the United States for spending on average $3 billion a year to alleviate AIDS in sub-Saharan Africa, and indeed it is a step in the right direction. Yet this paltry amount compared to what we spend on defense is threatened by a battle cry to cut the federal budget. East Africans recognize that North Americans are kind and generous people. Kenyans often told us that they simply wished that the U.S. government were as kind and generous as the American people.

A mother in South America was asked which of her ten children she favored the most, and she replied, "The one who needs me the most." Our Church and faith call us to a "preferential option for the poor." A "preferential option for the poor" may seem to favor some and ignore others, but what it emphasizes is that we must be ready to assist those in greater need as our mother/father God above does for her own children and as Zacchaeus realizes for himself. This change of behavior challenges us not only to look at our government systems but also our own behaviors. Zacchaeus did give half of his possessions to the poor, but most importantly he sought out a relationship and had a meal with Jesus. We can do this when we seek out relationships that might be uncomfortable for us.

Recently, a friend at church shared a story about walking through the streets of Chicago and passing a homeless man. As he passed, he told the man, "Sorry, I don't have anything to give you." The man, in frustration, responded: "A smile costs nothing." We all—poor, wealthy, sick, healthy, young, or old—have something to give. This self-giving was evident in our Kenyan neighbors who saved our Christmas dinner and modeled the giving spirit we see in Zacchaeus in the Gospel today. We begin with ourselves and then must continue that change in our relationships and move for change in our world.

Thirty-Second Sunday in Ordinary Time

Fr. Thomas Burns, MM

Peru

Second Maccabees 7:1–2, 9–14; Psalm 17:1, 5–6, 8, 15;
Second Thessalonians 2:16–3:5; Luke 20:27–38 or 20:27, 34–38

"Now he is God not of the dead but of the living . . ."
—*Luke 20:38*

Over seventy years ago, just before World War II, there were only 600,000 people in Lima and no one on the sand dunes in the Southern Cone of Lima where I have lived since 1974. Today, close to 1,300,000 people live on these dunes and Lima is a city of close to nine million! After the war, peasants from all over the country migrated to Lima looking for jobs and education for their children so that they could forge a better future for their families. They were poor, and for most of them, Spanish was a second language. In the beginning these young families had to live in dreadful circumstances, crowded into one-room hovels in the poorest parts of the city center.

But on Christmas Eve 1954 a sudden burst of light broke into their bleak situation: a few thousand people "invaded" the sand dunes in the desert of south Lima and took over its barren landscape. That "conquest of space" was the beginning of Lima's Southern Cone communities. This was the first major "invasion" in the history of Peru (and perhaps of Latin America). These migrations and invasions were generally met with intolerance from Lima's middle and upper class of mostly European origin; they often treated the migrants with disrespect, discrimination, and even contempt.

In today's Gospel the dynamics are somewhat similar: Jesus, an itinerant preacher and artisan from Galilee, arrives in Jerusalem. He is accompanied by his disciples, mostly fishermen or peasants. For the first time, Jesus and his followers come face to face with some Sadducees—mostly well-to-do merchants and rivals of the Pharisees for leadership in the Jerusalem community. Here, however, the Sadducees join their Pharisee rivals in opposition to this upstart preacher from the provinces.

The Sadducees accepted as legitimate only the Pentateuch (the first five books of the Bible), and they denied the resurrection. This life was the only life there was, and their riches were the proof that they were blessed by God. For them, life was to be lived in the present and enjoyed to its fullest. Jesus, on the other hand, was preaching that the Reign of God, promised by the prophets, had arrived: he was casting out devils, curing the sick, and even forgiving sins. He boldly announced that he had come to bring good news to the poor and oppressed and to announce the year of the Lord—a time of liberation from and forgiveness of debts. His preaching included the resurrection of the dead and eternal life as integral elements. Jesus' message gave hope to the poor and was a direct challenge to the snobbery, condescension, and complacency of the Sadducees. This is why they use the scriptures to ridicule the notion of the resurrection.

Jesus accepts the challenge and uses a key passage from the Pentateuch to respond. He cites Exodus 3:14, where God reveals his name to Moses in order to convince him to go to the people to let them know that their cries for help have been heard. God reveals concern for the harsh treatment they received under Egypt and promises to lead them to a land flowing with milk and honey. To convince Moses God introduces Godself as Yahweh and tells Moses, "Thus you shall say to the Israelites, 'The Lord, the God of your ancestors, the God of Abraham, the God of Isaac, and the God of Jacob, has sent me to you.'" And then Jesus adds, "Now he is God not of the dead, but of the living; for to him all of them are alive." God promised to an enslaved people both "a land of milk and honey" and the resurrection of the dead for all who believe. These messages of hope respond to the literal hunger for full life experienced by the poorest of the poor.

It is this hope that years ago encouraged the people of Peru to "invade" these sand dunes in the south of Lima to forge a new future. Far from the life of promise in a land of milk and honey, they have lived through a debt crisis and a cholera epidemic; they have lost jobs and the value of their hard-earned money, while repaying a national debt from which they never benefited. They have also endured a twenty-year internal war of terror and repression—but they still have hope and continue the struggle. It has been and continues to be a struggle for them, but it is this faith that keeps them going. For some life has improved a great deal, while for most, they give thanks to God that their lives are improving little by little, every year.

It is this same faith in the God of Life and Jesus' promise of the Kingdom that motivates the migration of my neighbors' children to other lands including the United States and Europe in search of a better life. As we know, this has caused a reaction of rejection and discrimination on the part of many not only in the United States but also in other lands. It makes me wonder whether this is a question, in the words of Yogi Berra, of "*déjà vu* all over again." If so, where do we stand? With the Sadducees or with Jesus, who said, "I was a stranger and you welcomed me"? There is no easy answer to this question but we follow Jesus' example and work to resolve our differences and bring good news to the poor.

Thirty-Third Sunday in Ordinary Time

David Kane, Maryknoll lay missioner

Brazil and Washington, D.C.

Malachi 3:19–20a; Psalm 98:5–9; Second Thessalonians 3:7–12;
Luke 21:5–19

*"As for these things that you see, the days will come when not one
stone will be left upon another; all will be thrown down."*
—*Luke 21:6*

I have heard people use parts of scripture like today's Gospel
to describe a terrible End Times doctrine, which portrays a
future of great suffering and destruction of Earth. Some have
even used these ideas to explain and support wars in the Middle East, saying that if these wars help to bring Jesus back
more quickly (by fulfilling the End Time prophecies), they
may actually be good. This is a dangerous misreading of the
Bible in my opinion. Today's readings show that we should
not be passively waiting for the end of Earth, but be actively
working to help bring about God's kingdom ". . . on Earth as
it is in Heaven."

In each of the synoptic Gospels, Jesus is portrayed as pre-
dicting that this destruction will happen soon. "Truly I tell
you, this generation will not pass away until all things have
taken place" (Luke 21:32). Clearly, almost two thousand
years later, we have to acknowledge that this statement cannot
be interpreted literally. Yet throughout those two millennia,
groups of Christians have withdrawn from society in expectation of the immediate coming of Jesus. At the turn of the millennia, numerous groups thought the end was coming. Again

in 2012, we saw other groups doing the same due to the end of a long cycle in the Mayan calendar.

Paul's letter today responds directly to this concept of waiting for an imminent end. In the letter, Paul addresses a specific problem confronting the Thessalonian community at that time: a number of followers had stopped working in anticipation of what they thought was the rapidly approaching end of time and second coming of Jesus. The letter was written around 70 C.E., about one generation after Jesus' prediction, so many had given up working to simply wait for the second coming. The growing number of idle people in the community was starting to lead to gossip, rumors, and infighting within the community.

When Paul writes, "Anyone unwilling to work should not eat," it was not a general exhortation to all the unemployed. He was specifically referring to those who had stopped working to wait for Jesus. Especially at a time like today, when levels of unemployment are so high around the world, Paul would have compassion for those who want to work but are unable to find employment. His words should not be used to imply a lack of compassion for unemployed workers.

So what are we to do while waiting for the second coming? Paul urges us to "work quietly and to earn [our] own living," while Jesus points out that by "your endurance you will gain your souls." They are telling us to continue in our work to help bring about God's kingdom "on Earth as it is in heaven." It could be, as some argue, that God's will is to rain down fire and brimstone to destroy the beautiful planet God created with such care, but that idea doesn't ring true to me. I am more of the opinion that God's will is more like Isaiah's New Earth, as described toward the end of his book:

> *For I am about to create new heavens and a new*
> *earth. . . . No more shall the sound of weeping be*
> *heard in it. . . . No more shall there be in it an infant*
> *that lives but a few days, or an old person who does*
> *not live out a lifetime; for one who dies at a hundred*
> *will be considered a youth, and one who falls short*
> *of a hundred will be considered accursed. They shall*
> *build houses and inhabit them; they shall plant vine-*
> *yards and eat their fruit. They shall not build and*
> *another inhabit; they shall not plant and another eat.*
> —Isaiah 65:17–21

Our goals are also clearly spelled out in Matthew's description of final judgment: Those who feed the hungry, give drink to the thirsty, clothe the naked, invite the stranger, and visit those who are sick or in prison will be chosen (Matthew 25:34–36). By doing these things and serving those facing the greatest difficulties, we create a loving community, a New Earth, where all people are able to have dignified work to support their own sustenance, where no one is excluded. This is the important work that Jesus has called us to, not to wait idly for Jesus to return.

Feast of Christ the King

Fr. James Kroeger, MM

Manila, Philippines

Second Samuel 5:1–3; Psalm 122:1–5; Colossians 1:12–20;
Luke 23:35–43

The soldiers also mocked him, coming up and offering him sour wine, and saying, "If you are the King of the Jews, save yourself!" There was also an inscription over him, "This is the King of the Jews."   —Luke 23:36–38

In September 2010, during his apostolic journey to the United Kingdom, Pope Benedict XVI addressed members of Parliament and a great gathering of men and women in public life from across Britain. The September 17 address was given in Westminster Hall, a historical location whose walls have echoed with many great events of British history. The trial of Saint Thomas More occurred in that very place; he was condemned to death for refusing to follow the rebellion of King Henry VIII against papal authority on divorce. Thomas More adhered to God and his personal conscience; his final words on the scaffold were: "The King's good servant, but God's first."

Benedict XVI noted: "The dilemma which faced More in those difficult times, the perennial question of the relationship between what is owed to Caesar and what is owed to God, allows me the opportunity to reflect with you briefly on the proper place of religious belief within the political process." The pope noted how "Britain has emerged as a pluralist democracy which places great value on the freedom of speech, freedom of political affiliation and respect for the rule of law, with a strong sense of the individual's rights and duties, and of the equality of all citizens before the law."

The pope continued: "While couched in different language, Catholic social teaching has much in common with this approach, in its overriding concern to safeguard the unique dignity of every human person, created in the image and likeness of God, and in its emphasis on the duty of civil authority to foster the common good." Benedict spoke on the "legitimate role of religion in the public square." He also noted: "I would suggest that the world of reason and the world of faith—the world of secular rationality and the world of religious belief—need one another and should not be afraid to enter into a profound and ongoing dialogue, for the good of our civilization."

One can validly assert that Thomas More, in his day, deeply understood that religious faith, personal convictions, freedom of conscience, and commitment to Christ's values in both personal and public life are all integral parts of claiming that Christ is truly one's King. More served as the lord chancellor of England but resigned rather than sign an oath declaring Henry's marriage to Catherine of Aragon invalid. He was imprisoned in 1534 and beheaded on July 6, 1535. Significantly, his letters from prison in the Tower of London reveal a deep devotion to the suffering Christ. Indeed, for More, Christ was King, his suffering-crucified King.

Today's Gospel from Luke (23:35–43), chosen precisely for the Feast of Christ the King, portrays Jesus as a crucified king. Christ's kingship, in the Christian perspective, is linked with a "kingly" vision of being a humble and suffering servant, a vision that unites Thomas More, Benedict XVI, and all individual Christians—you and I included!

If asked what movie I have seen most frequently in my whole life, I would have to reply, *A Man for All Seasons.* This 1960s film was based on a play written by Robert Bolt. In explaining his choice of Thomas More for the drama, Bolt gave this rationale: "A man takes an oath only when he wants to commit himself quite exceptionally to the statement, when he wants to make an identity between the truth of it and his own virtue; he offers himself as a guarantee." Bolt believes that "a clear sense of the self can crystallize only around something transcendental." Thus, More becomes "a Christian saint, as a hero of selfhood."

Thomas More explains this radical self-awareness, faith, and commitment to his daughter Margaret when she visits him in prison. "When a man takes an oath, Meg, he's holding his own self in his own hands. Like water. And if he opens his fingers then—he needn't hope to find himself again. Some men are capable of this, but I'd be loath to think your father one of them."

The feast of Christ the King, coming at the end of the liturgical year, is a wonderful opportunity for reflection on the depth of our acceptance of Christ as our King, our crucified King. Does he truly rule our lives, our thoughts, our public and private morality, our desires? Has his reign in our lives transformed our values and deepened our relationships? Pope Benedict XVI was asking similar questions of British society— and the world. Thomas More gave his answer—with his life. Jesus had truly become his King! In deep faith, More could even say to his executioner: "Friend, be not afraid of your office. You send me to God."

Each day as Christians say the Our Father, we pray: "Your Kingdom come!" And, what kind of kingdom do we work, pray, and suffer for? As stated so beautifully in the Preface of today's Mass, we ask God to establish "an eternal and universal kingdom, a kingdom of truth and life, a kingdom of holiness and grace, a kingdom of justice, love, and peace." O crucified-risen Lord, may your kingdom come!

Contributors

Scripture Index